FRAG
in BLOOM

Cultivating the Scented Garden
Throughout the Year

ANN LOVEJOY

SASQUATCH BOOKS
SEATTLE

0 9 8 7 6 5 4 3 2
Cover and interior design: Virginia Hand
Cover photograph: Lynne Harrison
Interior color photographs: Mark Lovejoy
Interior illustrations: Jean Emmons
Copy editing: Alice Copp Smith
Composition: Virginia Hand

Library of Congress Cataloging in Publication Data
Lovejoy, Ann, 1951–
      Fragrance in Bloom / Ann Lovejoy.
          p.   cm. -- (Cascadia gardening series)
      Includes bibliographical references (p.   ) and index.
      ISBN 1-57061-026-6
1. Fragrance in Bloom. 2. Aromatic plants. I. Title. II. Series.
SB454.3.F7L68   1995
635.9'68--dc20   94-42439
                                        CIP

Sasquatch Books
1008 Western Avenue
Seattle, Washington 98104
(206) 467-4300
books@sasquatchbooks.com
http://www.sasquatchbooks.com

Other books by Ann Lovejoy:
Seasonal Bulbs
The Border in Bloom
The Year in Bloom
Three Years in Bloom: A Garden-Keeper's Journal

Contents

To Gary Luke

That rarest of creatures, a patient visionary.

Introduction

*T*his book is the slowly ripened fruit of many years' garden making. Over time, that lengthy, complex process involved an enormous amount of plant selection and rejection. Some of my experiments led to astonishingly sweet successes, while others resulted in (on occasion, notable) nonfragrant failures. My early trials were rather fumbling attempts to figure out how to put fragrant plants together in satisfying (or at least relatively pleasant) combinations. I innocently thought it would be as simple as plunking a fruity rose next to a sugary clematis (or peony, or whatever) and enjoying the happy result. Often this straightforward approach works beautifully, but at times, it leads to surprisingly nasty results.

We humans are able to distinguish some ten thousand distinct smells. This is only a fraction of what a good bloodhound can recognize, but it nonetheless encompasses a huge spectrum of olfactory experiences. The complications, however, arise less from the sheer size of the scent palette than from the fact that many scents are mutable. They can alter because of age or time of day, with the season or the weather, because of soil or cultural care. What's more, we, too, are mutable. Our perceptions change along with our moods, so that what smells good one day may smell wretched when we have a cold, or aren't in love, or have a cash flow problem.

When I looked for solid information about fragrance, I ended up consulting chemistry or biology books rather than horticultural ones. They were rarely directly helpful, but they did explain certain phenomena. Plants that alter their scents from day to night often have several pollinators—some day feeders, others nocturnal. Some perfumes need to mix with air before they are detectable by the human nose; sniff the flower and smell nothing, but step back ten feet, and Wow!

Although a number of gardening books discuss fragrant plants in general, few mention the way floral fragrances can change over time, or how they mingle or clash. Even fewer books discuss using fragrant plants in concert, and none that I know of address the concept of deliberately creating sequential fragrance effects. This book attempts to do all these things, not in a didactic way but in the adventurous spirit that motivates all experimental gardening.

For my first few years as a gardener, my goal was just to learn how to keep my plants alive and happy. After a while, my vision expanded with my skills, and other goals appeared as my horticultural horizons broadened. I began trying to put my plants together in ways that pleased both me and them. Next, I wanted to have something in flower or fruit or splendid leaf on any given day of the year. Somewhere along the way, I began wanting to have a garden that smelled as wonderful as the gardens I remembered from childhood. After a bit, that goal too expanded into the hope of creating sequences of sumptuous smells all year long. This last ambition is most easily achieved when we give in to plant lust as often as possible. Just by bringing a wide range of plants into our gardens, we can almost guarantee that our gardens will smell good. We can improve the odds by deliberately choosing species and cultivars that are deliciously fragrant, then combining them in ways that smell terrific. This book is intended to streamline the process so that your garden can quickly become a bower of fragrance as well as of bloom.

Here in the maritime Northwest—from southern British Columbia to southern Oregon, west of the Cascade Mountains—those of us who garden are in the enviable position of having to choose amongst an overwhelming variety of plants that will thrive with very little coaxing. Whether we work on heavy, acid clay or sandy soils, we nonetheless can select from literally thousands of excellent plants that will appreciate the settings and conditions our particular garden presents. This luxury of choice can make it hard to discipline ourselves, but it also makes it easy to find a replacement for any plant that doesn't appreciate the setting we have to offer.

We can also be incredibly picky about what we choose to plant in our gardens in the first place. We can hold out for trees that offer elegance of form, winter beauty, and appropriate size in maturity. We can require mannerly vines with lovely foliage, flowers, and fruit. We can reject any border shrub that doesn't have multiple beauties over three or four seasons. We can demand that our perennials be as attractive in habit and leaf as in flower. What's more, we can ask that a large proportion of all of the above be fragrant, yet we will still have far too many fine choices to cram into even a large garden.

Whether you are adding plants to an established garden or just getting started with a new one, this book will help to guide you through that selection process so that you end up with plants that are regionally appropriate and beautiful as well as marvelously scented. Clearly, it's not possible to mention all of the fragrant plant possibilities in a book of this size. However, it is very possible to broaden the range of what's being grown in Northwestern gardens. To this end, you will find mention here of the most fragrant forms of many old favorites, but you will also find an introduction to uncommon but easily grown fragrant plants that deserve greater popularity. I hope that the descriptions of their merits will pique your interest, tempting you to try some of these less-familiar plants. A garden is a wonderful place to take risks, for while at worst we may lose a (usually) replaceable plant, at best we gain a friendly, sometimes lifelong, garden companion. Certainly, we can and should have our first plant loves with us—who would be without lilacs, or roses, or lilies? However, when we take a flyer on a complete unknown, whether it be a *Fothergilla gardenii* or a chocolate cosmos or a winter honeysuckle, we may enrich both our gardens and our lives. Really, this is pretty much a sure thing, for the plants discussed here will bring you not only olfactory pleasure but also the joy—rivaled by few others in life—of discovering new plant loves.

Our usually benign climate allows us to be active in our gardens throughout most, if not all, of the year. Discovering plants that spill their scents in autumn or winter or earliest spring expands our enjoyment manyfold. Each chapter in this book presents a number of deliciously fragrant plants that perform in a certain season. If, for instance, you want to reward yourself as you weed through sodden borders in January, you will find a goodly assortment of sweet treats to choose amongst in Chapter Five, "Winter Scents." If you entertain a good deal in summer, Chapter Six, "Night-Fragrant Plants," will be a useful guide as you select plants in spring for deck or patio containers.

The experience of fragrance is as quirky and personal as that of color, and there is no way to set out firm and fast rules for appreciating either one. However, I would like to suggest the possibilities of another delightfully pleasant endeavor, that of learning to use fragrant plants in concert. In organizing the resulting living perfumes, we create unique experiences and memorable impressions for ourselves and others. This soon becomes a creative outlet that can provide as much pleasure as developing colorist effects in the garden. Indeed, while fragrance gardening makes an enchanting supplement to colorist work, it is also a keen delight in its own right. What's more, it is one that can be equally enjoyed by anybody, at any level of expertise. Young or old, keen gardener or not interested in gardening at all, everybody enjoys the delightful smells that emanate from the fragrance garden all year long. Best of all, fragrance gardening is just plain fun—which should, after all, be a major part of the garden-making experience.

—*Ann Lovejoy*
Bainbridge Island, Washington

Chapter
One

1

CREATING
FRAGRANCE
EFFECTS
IN THE
GARDEN

Strolling through the garden on an early summer morning, tea mug in hand, the gardener is greeted by the intensely green smell of dew-spangled lawn, the mild fragrance of opening daylilies, the mellow scent of spearmint brushed by trailing fingers. Midday brings the wafting, powerful perfumes of rose and mignonette as well as the sharper odors of pungent santolina or aromatic lavender. Evening-scented stocks and tobaccos arrive with twilight and linger long into the night. Despite such *richesse*, fragrance—most especially the deliberately orchestrated fragrance effect—is a largely underused garden component.

In part, this diffidence reflects the fact that humans experience smells in vastly different ways. Some of us love the musty sweetness of privet, while for others it is an annoying allergen. The bitter, biting aroma of chrysanthemums or nasturtiums may be attractive to me, yet repellent to you. Thanks to literary associations, some of us find the smell of sweet violets swooningly romantic, yet to others they speak only of cheap perfume. The first trick, therefore, in successfully incorporating fragrant plants into our gardens is to discover which smells we actively enjoy and to sift out those we find distasteful.

In order to do this properly, it is necessary (in terms of good research, you understand—not simply greed) to buy large quantities of unknown plants that are said to be fragrant or at least agreeable-smelling. Once you begin this pleasant indulgence, you'll very soon connect up with that small but impassioned group of gardeners who grow plants chiefly for their scents. Indeed, there are even specialty nurseries that cater specifically to such gardeners.

Though mere profusion can create an overwhelming bewilderment of scents, a well-orchestrated series of fragrances can delightfully amplify our pleasure

in experiencing a garden. If this kind of orchestration is rare, it is largely because gardening literature offers relatively few mentions of scent and no clear directions for how to weave it into patterns. We may choose our roses as much for fragrance as for flower color, but color, shape, and texture (all of which can be communicated by a catalog photograph) are far more common reasons for growing specific plants. Generally, too, when we admire a garden scene, we know how to make mental notes about color effects, companionable plant relationships, the way the beds flow about the house. We notice handsome garden structures, interesting architectural features, all sorts of details relating to the physical arrangement of garden elements. Similarly tangible considerations tend to occupy us when we plan our own gardens, so that, most often, fragrance effects come about by accident rather than by design.

If fragrance is seldom among the gardener's first concerns, it should not be the last, for smells—all kinds of smells—play a subtle, reinforcing role in creating the ambience we want. Gentle herbal scents encourage stressed bodies to relax. Bracingly aromatic odors invigorate dull moods. Certain perfumes unfailingly entice us to abandon ourselves to enjoyment, while others seem exhilarating or fascinatingly mysterious. As our plant collections expand, we learn more about the qualities and particularities of our favorites. It becomes enormous fun to plan out fragrance effects, deliberately creating a stimulating sequence of scents to greet us as we walk. In one area, we may intermingle a series of gentle scents, which combine into a living perfume. Elsewhere, delicate fragrances build up to stronger

Certain perfumes unfailingly entice us to abandon ourselves to pleasure, while others seem exhilarating or fascinatingly mysterious. ∾

ones, which are then tempered by sharp or astringent neighbors. We learn to use distinctly contrasting scents for refreshment, pairing the spicy, yarrowlike aroma of lavender cotton (*Santolina chamaecyparissus*) with the velvety jungle perfume of petunias, or mixing dreamy mignonette with brisk lemon thyme.

Since the experience of fragrance is highly personal, it's useful to record in your garden journal your own reactions to both new and familiar scents. Over time, you can generate lists of plants that you perceive as smelling pungent or bitter, sickly sweet or sumptuous, aromatic or astringent. Experiment, too, with combinations of scent types—do you love pine and lemon but hate sage and roses? Keep notes of your impressions, so you can see whether your likes and dislikes are seasonally influenced. Be prepared for them to change over time, for skills are often sharpened and refined by exercise. As we begin to pay more and more careful attention to scents, we become better able to appreciate subtle qualities that usually go unnoticed. Leave room to amend your reactions; you will be fascinated by your own expanding abilities as time goes by. Arranged by season as well as by plant type (perennial, shrub, and so forth), these personalized lists will become an excellent resource when you begin creating fragrance arrangements within the garden.

It's a good idea to build in a few rest stops along the fragrant path, places where no single scent demands our attention. Once we become really awake to plant perfumes, it is quite easy to get carried away. Before long, we are passionately adding any and all sorts of scented ingredients to our garden. The result introduces us to an important lesson: more isn't always better. Delightful as each fragrance may be on its own, in combination fragrances can lead up to an olfactory overdose. Too much sweetness becomes cloying, a glut of mystery leaves us dazed, an excess of passion can intoxicate. After a while, in self-defense, our poor noses simply stop working.

Alternating vivid scents with understated ones helps restore our ability to discern nuances that are obliterated by a more constant barrage. (The same principle underlies the practice of offering a light, palate-cleansing sorbet between the courses of an elaborate meal.)

Nostalgic scents are particularly effective mood makers, carrying us back to childhood or especially happy times and places. Perhaps the fragrance of black locust on warm evening air in late spring reminds you of your first love, or the heavy perfume of musk roses makes you hear your favorite grandmother's voice. I have a friend for whom the smell of boxwood (which reminds me only of male cat spray) is blissfully transporting because his happiest childhood vacations were spent in a garden edged with boxwood hedges. The faintly moldy sweetness of hawthorn may recall a blissful English spring, while lavender and rosemary evoke the south of France. A large part of the charm of garden making lies in the gardener's ability to create (or re-create) scenes and settings that inspire both personal comfort and active pleasure.

In my own garden, certain fragrance effects are designed to reward my faithful labors during the off seasons. Under a tangled kerria hedge (which requires serious annual pruning) lurk several sorts of sweet box (*Sarcococca* spp.). Invisible behind a wall of perennials all summer, in winter they offer warm cookie scents of honey and vanilla from January into March. The backs of my deep borders are inaccessible in summer, so I tend them from late fall into spring. Those shrubby border backs hold lots of late and early bloomers, many of them wonderfully perfumed. Wintersweet (*Chimonanthus praecox*), primrose-scented witch hazels (*Hamamelis* spp.), and sugary boxleaf azara (*Azara microphylla*) all ease the ardors of cold-weather gardening with their sumptuous smells.

A rival delight is to arrange seasonally changing arrays of fragrant plants around important garden sitting areas. We may embower a favorite bench in especially sweet-smelling roses, from sunny little 'Rise 'n' Shine' to the enormous apricot confections of 'Just Joey', a hybrid tea with an excess of everything. The picnic table can be surrounded by large pots of sweet-smelling things: fragrant shrubs and bulbs in winter and spring, sweet alyssum, fizzy green mignonette, and petunias in summer. We might wreath the terrace in fragrant clematis and honeysuckles that bloom in sequence through much of the year. In my garden, the garden seats we like to use on summer evenings are backed by pots of the golden, peachy daturas called 'Charles Grimaldi'. Not only do they look exactly like Ginger Rogers's swirling skirts, but their spilling night fragrance is mildly euphoric—an uncommon quality that promotes sparkling repartee (or quite a good illusion thereof).

Create seasonally changing sequences of fragrance near paths and doorways by combining power-fully fragrant plants in pots. ❧

The easiest and most rewarding site for fragrance experiments is a sunny, open patio or terrace. Given such a site, it's a snap to create a wide variety of fragrance effects to be enjoyed from chair or hammock. The narrow cracks between the pavers can be crammed with creeping mints and thymes, which release their mingled scents at our every step. Lemon and orange, rose and ginger, apple and bergamot scented mints are all good scramblers that withstand a good deal of foot pressure, while pennyroyal positively relishes being stepped on. Where summers are actually hot (inland parts of Oregon come to mind), mints will appreciate a bit of shade, which may come from nearby shrubs or trees, large pots, or even outdoor furniture (grow them under a patio table, for instance). Sun-loving thymes smell pleasingly culinary: lemon thyme has an especially attractive, bright edge to its scent, while caraway-scented thyme reminds my nose of herb bread.

Pots of herbs and scented geraniums can be stood about on terrace or deck in complementary clusters, ready to yield up their combined fragrances to any passing hand. Citrus-scented fruit sage (*Salvia dorisiana*) mixes delightfully with the mild bite of peppermint and sparkly lemon balm. Balsam-scented hyssop and spice-tea-like bee balm (*Monarda*) make pleasing fragrance companions, as do rose- and lime-scented geraniums with pineapple sage. Lavender, astringent artemisias, and spicy clove pinks make up another splendid combination that is readily roused by the heat of the sun on leaf and petal.

For me, the smell of sun-warmed pine needles mingled with lemon blossom, thyme, and rosemary is especially evocative, recalling lazy Mediterranean summers. In my rather shady Northwestern garden, this is not an easy effect to recapture, but I have spent several seasons happily trying. My current project involves tucking a small, stone-flagged terrace beneath a high-limbed white pine in the sunniest corner of our garden. Though I can't reliably manage genuine lemon blossom (our wood-heated, elderly farmhouse gets too cold in winter to keep potted plants happy), herbs like lemon balm (*Melissa officinalis*) and shrubby lemon verbena (*Aloysia triphylla*) play much the same role. The cracks of the paving are stuffed with thymes, and several sprawling rosemaries are sizing up nicely at each edge. In Greece or Provence or southern Italy, the mingled odors would arrive unsought; here, I have to go about brushing this plant and that to release their scents, and the fitful sun rarely warms the pine sufficiently to fill the air with its sharp smell. Still, it's not a bad approximation.

While developing olfactory themes can be as playful and satisfying a pursuit for the garden maker as color work, it is worth remembering that fragrances can be variable. Like plant size and flower color or timing, plant smells can be affected by a wide range of factors. Weather and soil account for a good deal of such variation, but other, less obvious influences may be at work as well. A plant that smells wonderful in one garden may disappoint in another, despite few apparent differences of soil or site or situation. This means we can't always rely on other people's lists of successful fragrance effects, but must develop our own. Fortunately, this is a delightful pursuit, one that can engage our active interest for many years as we discover our own particular fragrant paths.

*Chapter
Two*

2

THE
SCENTS OF
SPRING

March, April, May

Everywhere in the world, spring smells browny-green, like warming earth and growing grass. Here in the maritime Northwest, the first burst of that concentrated essence may arrive in the middle of winter. One day, a gentle chinook blows in, carrying warm, wet air from the south. Immediately, people's faces soften along with the garden soil; indoors and out, everybody looks rejuvenated and revitalized. A gardener with enough leisure could actually watch plants respond to that enticing warmth as well, for early bloomers like Greek windflower (*Anemone blanda*) can put on an inch of top growth in a single winter day when the weather is right.

Those precious January thaws are often followed by February squalls and arctic cold fronts, but the promise has been given. In a mild year, the storms will be brief and the temperatures will never plummet enough to slow the arrival of spring. Winter fades away and spring slips in without much fuss. While those years are often the best for gardening, they are somehow less satisfying than the difficult years when dramatic weather provokes endless garden tragedies. On some primal level, we expect winter to be hard. When it is, we appreciate spring all the more for the sheer contrast provided by fierce winds or killing cold. After such experiences, we are definitely ready for March, when the vernal equinox signals the true arrival of spring. Good year or bad, it arrives with enough ebullience to satisfy our deepest cravings for growth and greenness.

In my garden, March sweeps in with a host of fragrant plants in her train. Primroses of many kinds are tucked under every tree and bush, where they can be enjoyed during the second half of the garden year. Often, they bloom sporadically from autumn through winter, providing a sparse but constant handful of sweet-smelling blossoms for the table. In March, they are solid masses of flower, as are the sweet violets, which spill their soapy scent even more generously when asked to tough it out in

dry, rooty places. The sailor-blue scillas that bloom in early spring smell like ripe grapes, while jonquils and the old double daffodils like 'Pencrebar' have a robust, full-bodied sweetness reminiscent of the paperwhites we force for indoor bloom in winter. Fluffy yellow belled spikes of shrubby Oregon grape (*Mahonia aquifolium*) smell like lemons mixed with honey and spice. They are always abuzz with the earliest bees, who seem to find the pollen as delicious as the scent. The astonishing, piercing scent of Japanese plum carries well on still-cool spring air, along with the insinuating night fragrance of laurel spurge (*Daphne laureola*).

April showers awaken a hundred heady scents, from daphnes and viburnums to the sheer romance of hyacinths. Single early tulips and the cottage kind are often fragrant, as are many of the midseason daffodils. Sweet alyssum begins to open in pavement cracks and warm wall crannies, while magnolias and fruit trees pour out their splendid scents. All sorts of midspring bulb blossoms have pleasant perfumes, notably narcissus like 'Thalia' and 'Geranium'. Midspring also brings plenty of fragrant border shrubs to use in companionable garden groupings. Such plantings are especially rewarding when chosen and arranged so that their scents are as complementary as the colors of their flowers.

Sprinkle seeds of sweet scented alyssum, stocks, dianthus, and mignonette along walkways, steps, and into the gaps of garden walls.

❧

May brings lilac, with its rich, penetrating fragrance, as well as the sharp, clean scent of brooms and the heavy, honey-and-hops (or honey-and-mildew, depending on your nose) smell of hawthorn. Sweet woodruff spreads in lovely, scented pools by day, melding at night with the caressing scent of dame's rocket (*Hesperis matronalis*). Late tulips and the splendidly sweet poet's narcissus mingle with early peonies and the first roses,

their odors mixing in a delightful garden perfume. By month's end, simply walking into the garden creates an olfactory sonata, and every little breeze changes the composition.

As the days draw out, the lingering spring evenings are the perfect time to simply be in the garden, drinking it in with all our senses. Bird song and flower fragrance, evening sun and the smell of cut grass all blend into an essential entity that transcends sight, sound, and sensation. When we sit quietly and open ourselves to it, we truly are experiencing being within the garden.

Oregon Grape

One of my first spring bloomers is planted so far back in a deep bed that it would probably be overlooked were it not for its alluring scent. Tall and upright, decked with glossy, evergreen, hollylike leaves, *Mahonia* × *media* 'Charity' (6–10') looks like a large version of our native Oregon grape, *M. aquifolium*. A cross between two Asian species—*M. japonica* and a lovely, long-leaved Chinese cousin, *M. lomarifolia*—it is a little more tender than our native plants and needs a slightly shady, sheltered spot to give its best performance. Protected from harsh wind, it grows into a powerfully sculptural evergreen that looks terrific all year long. It produces fat bloom spikes studded with warm yellow florets in early spring, permeating the garden with honey and citrus. Underplant its skirts with fragrant daffodils like 'Thalia' to intensify the sweetness. (See also Chapter Five, "Winter Scents.")

Grape Hyacinths

Sea-blue grape hyacinth, *Muscari armeniacum* (6–10"), is another favorite fragrant and early bloomer. The common name reflects the ripe-

fruit sweetness of these ardent little bulbs. Grape hyacinths are rugged plants that prosper in meadows and wild gardens, needing only decent soil and a few hours of daily sunlight to keep them thriving. The usual species is charming but overeager, and should never be planted amongst delicate plants, which it will swamp without compunction. Those bright blue spikes are delightful from March through April, but the foliage becomes flopsy by May, smothering anything in its range. To avoid this, trim the leaves back by half when they start to tumble. An even simpler solution is to plant grape hyacinths where they can wander as they please, perhaps between the garage and the recycling bins, or under established rhododendrons.

Though not all forms of this happy creature are fragrant, those found in older gardens nearly always are. If you can't find sweet ones at a nursery, beg a clump from a neighbor blessed with a fragrant form, or order scented forms from a specialty catalog. The baby-boy blue (or Cambridge blue, to a Brit) *M. a.* 'Cantab', has a very pretty scent, while 'Heavenly Blue' has a saturated scent as potent as the summer-sky blue of its bells. These selected forms are not quite as thuggy as the straight species, but they are still too quick to spread for placement in most borders. Let them colonize happily in the long grass of orchard or meadow, ringed around mature trees, or rowed out beneath a thick hedge. Should the clumps become overcrowded, dig them up as soon as the flowers fade, then divide them into smaller groups. Encircle a fragrant lavender-blue azalea or a golden-leaved mock orange (*Philadelphus coronarius* 'Aureus') for a sumptuously perfumed display.

Other fragrant grape hyacinths are not so easy to find, and they need rather different conditions in order to thrive. Late-spring-blooming musk hyacinth, *M. muscarimi* [*M. moschatum*], is a plant for a sunny rock garden, where its leathery, almost succulent leaves can sprawl over

hot gravel. Its inflated green-and-white bells look much like blueberry blossoms, set sparsely around sturdy, sinuous stalks. Their musky sweetness has magical, mysterious depths, and while too much of this smell can be cloying, two or three spikes mixed into a little bouquet will scent a room fascinatingly.

Ambrosia hyacinths smell ambrosial indeed, like fresh fruit salad dressed with hazelnut liqueur. Tuck a few stalks into floral table decorations. ❧

Ambrosia hyacinth, *M. macrocarpum* [*ambrosiacum*], also likes a well-drained place in the sun. This one has pale purple buds that turn buttery, then open into narrow, lemon yellow flowers. They smell like fresh fruit salad with hazelnut liqueur poured over it, and a few stalks will make a remarkable contribution if tucked into the floral table decorations at a late-spring garden party. All grape hyacinths partner well with the sturdy scent of poet's narcissus and fragrant jonquils like 'Dove Wing'.

Hyacinths

idspring-blooming Dutch or florist's hyacinths have one of the strongest floral perfumes in the garden, as potent and far-reaching as any August lily. These colorful bulbs are forms of *Hyacinthus orientalis* (to 10"), a much-selected species that adapts very well to Northwestern garden conditions. They last longest in enriched soils that drain well, and appreciate annual applications of compost, soymeal or cottonseed meal, and aged manure each fall to keep their roots fed in winter. They like full sun, but will tolerate light or partial shade, so long as they are not grown in damp sites (where the bulbs are apt to rot). The dormant bulbs need to be kept dry, so tuck them under deciduous shrubs like *Daphne* × *burkwoodii*, where they can be protected from excess summer water. (The blue

ones look smashing beneath the short, coppery skirts of *Spiraea japonica* 'Gold Flame'.)

Most hyacinths will be smaller and less densely plumed after a few seasons, but that steady feeding in fall or early winter will keep them productive for many years. When well suited in terms of sun and company (or competition), hyacinths colonize as readily in enriched sandy soils as in heavy clay-based ones. Should a clump become too congested to bloom strongly, lift and divide the bulbs in late spring, resetting them in fresh compost or good garden soil for many happy returns. Hyacinths partner well with all sorts of compact border shrubs, in both color and scent. Pair white 'L'Innocence' hyacinths with rosy pink *Daphne odora* for a swooningly sweet combination, or set pale salmon 'Gypsy Queen' beneath a creamy yellow 'Moonlight' broom for a brisker one.

Daphne

A charming pair of midspring-blooming daphnes repeat their floral display in late summer or early autumn. *Daphne × burkwoodii* (to 4'), is a shapely, well furnished and staunchly upright little shrub that looks equally at home in a formal garden or a cottagey one. It is classified as semievergreen, which means that in a good year it looks great all winter. However, a harsh one will cause it to shed most of its leaves, and it behooves the gardener to relieve it of the remains, which otherwise look sadly bedraggled for months. Luckily, it will refurbish itself nicely come spring, when there will also be generous clusters of tubular flowers, creamy white shading to shell pink as they mature. Their intensely sweet odor needs a sharper-edged neighbor such as lavender cotton (*Santolina chamaecyparissus*). A clean, lightly scented broom like lavender-and-mauve 'Lilac Time' or pink-and-purple 'Munstead' will also make excellent

company for Burkwood daphne, both visually and to balance the sweetness.

In late spring, *Daphne retusa* (to 2½') is still going strong. This exceptional little shrub remains neat and handsome all year round. Happy plants bloom both in April and in August, producing fat little red fruits after each interesting event. Its wine purple buds open into white, pink-flushed flowers, small, but thickly clustered along the fleshy stems. It smells just as dazzling as its commoner cousin, winter daphne (*D. odora*), but is a shapelier, more refined and compact plant with smaller, more tapered leaves.

Fothergilla

*F*othergillas rank among the most choice and charming of deciduous shrubs, and I can't think why they are not more often grown. Mannerly and compact, these little witch hazel relatives fit gracefully into all kinds of gardens, large or small, formal or relaxed. Their large, rounded leaves make a bold counterpoint to billowy perennials and take on exceptional sunset tints in fall. In late winter or early spring, their curious little bottlebrush flowers tip each stem with silky white tassels. The larger form, *Fothergilla monticola*, reaches eight or ten feet in time, making a splendid transition between mature trees and garden beds and borders. Like rhododendrons, it prefers acid soils but dislikes wet feet. Ordinary, decent garden soil and a sunny site will keep a fothergilla happy for many years.

A smaller version, *F. gardenii* (to 4'), is covered all spring with fluffy little flowers that smell enticingly sweet, especially on warm days. Plant this near a *Daphne retusa* if you can, because the two scents combine deliciously, creating a sensory treat that's matched only by the mingled fragrances of apple blossom and the early-blooming rose called 'Canary Bird'.

Clematis

I used to swear that I would never have one of those cordless telephones that you can carry around with you. Part of the joy of being in the garden was not hearing the phone ring, not being endlessly on call. However, I have recently learned that these gadgets can add a new dimension of pleasure to being in the garden.

After a long, hard weekend of working in the garden, a friend called to remind me that appreciation is just as important as tidying. Linked by our telephones, we sat in our gardens together, sipping wine and talking about what we saw and smelled. My friend was certainly right in her observation, for despite much unfinished business, there was a great deal to admire. The borders were lush with glossy new growth, fresh and robust. The evening light was soft, the blue sky dappled with gilded clouds. Countless busy birds were twittering in the trees, and the air was rich with the living perfume of spring.

My friend Lindsay was waxing poetic about her anemone clematis, *Clematis montana* (to 30'), which pours out its astonishing perfume on warm evenings. Big, chalky flowers like single, four-petaled roses are held above the coppery young leaves, which come in trios on the winding, supple stems. The vanilla-with-a-hint-of-nutmeg scent builds slowly through the day, climaxing as the late-afternoon sun begins to sink.

This early bloomer is a lusty creature that can easily scale a Douglas fir in time. Lindsay's vine covers her solid Victorian porch, intertwined with the saw-

Put Clematis montana *on a sturdy trellis (the kind you'd offer a wisteria), drape it over a retaining wall, or let it clamber into a Douglas fir.* ❧

toothed, old gold leaves of golden hops (*Humulus lupulus* 'Aureus'). That's quite a combination, both visually and in terms of weight and volume, and not many garden trellises could bear such a burden.

My own *Clematis montana* is a warmer pink form called 'Alexander', which in five years has filled a gnarled, twisting old plum tree. This year, those questing tendrils are making their way into a neighboring holly, in which they will look very nice indeed. After that, there are a couple of tall blue spruces for it to acquire. When it does, this garden too will offer the combination of anemone clematis with golden hops, which already inhabits those spruces.

Apple Blossom

Lighter in quality than the scent of anemone clematis, the deliciously fresh, floral scent of apple blossoms also wanders nicely through the garden. This year, in late April, four or five apple trees were in bloom at once, joining the last of the plums, cherries, and pears. All of these are more or less fragrant, but none have the penetrating, romantic perfume of orchard apples.

Among the strongest scented are old-fashioned apples like 'King' and 'Lady Apple'. These are hard to find, except from specialty nurseries like Raintree in Oregon. Fortunately, certain widely available decorative crabapples smell very pleasant as well. Arnold crab, *Malus arnoldiana* (to 20'), bears heavy crops of sweet-scented rosy flowers that fade to cream, followed by fat little gold-and-crimson apple-ettes. *M. coronaria* 'Charlotte' gets a bit larger (to 30'), and is smothered in midspring under loads of tight double pink rosettes that have a remarkably pretty scent. Best of all is the Sargent crabapple, *M. sargentii* (to 12'), which not only carries masses of deliciously fragrant white flowers but offers splendid autumn leaf color as well. ('Charlotte' runs a fair second in that department too.)

Lilac

ilacs, too, have a traveling scent, especially the old-fashioned varieties found in the dooryards of elderly houses across the country. Modern hybrids are far showier in flower, but in fragrance, none rival plain *Syringa vulgaris* (to 20'). Actually, this old standard has several hundred not-so-plain offspring with plenty of perfume. Though they are usually called French hybrids, many were developed either in North America or in England. Some of this latter are especially good performers in the Pacific Northwest, where mild winters, cool spring nights, and overcast days encourage bacterial blights, mildews, and other interesting diseases on lilacs.

Northwestern gardeners are safest sticking with the single lilacs, for doubles tend to ball like roses in wet springs. When this happens, each promising bud grows grey with furry mold and the crop of flowers is sadly reduced. Good single forms abound, so take your nose to the nursery in April and May and discover your own favorites. Mine include clean white 'Vestale' as well as 'Alba', which has smaller flowers but is to me the sweetest of the whites. Deep purple 'Cavour' is a handsome thing, as is wine red 'Ludwig Spaeth', but the most delicious, Concord-grape purple I have ever seen is a newer one called 'Agincourt

Sargent crabapple is an excellent choice for small gardens, offering spring fragrance, summer fruit, autumn color, and an elegant winter silhouette. ∾

Choose lilacs as much for scent as for the color of their mid-spring flowers. ∾

Beauty'. Sky blue 'Firmament' is still among the cleanest of the blues, and has far more fragrance than any of the new hybrids. I am very fond of the soft, butter yellow 'Primrose', which has a soft, buttery scent to match, lighter yet spicier than old-fashioned lilacs. In general, the newer the hybrid, the flashier the flower but the fainter the scent (some do not even have a discernible fragrance, which is like having a scentless rose). For knock-out perfume, the older forms are still hands-down winners, for most of them are as potently delicious as their species parent, *S. vulgaris*.

To keep your lilac happy, plant it in the sunniest spot you can offer. Deep soil, well enriched with humus, will give young plants a great start, and you will enjoy good bloom in just a few seasons. That is, you will if you can resist the urge to perform the relentless overpruning that lilac seems to excite in many gardeners. Prune young lilacs lightly, if at all, letting them develop into multi-trunked shrubs rather than single-trunked trees. Most plants don't sucker badly unless they (quite rightly) feel themselves to be under attack, so lay off the pruners and give your plant a chance to get established before having at it. Older plants might be choked with suckers, which should be removed at the base to open up the heart of the plant to light and air. A couple of the oldest stems can be taken out every few years, but don't do too much at once, or the reaction will be worse than the original problem.

Lilacs really prefer alkaline soils, which are rare indeed west of the Cascades. In these parts, it's an excellent idea to add some dolomite or agricultural lime to the soil before planting lilacs. Lime can also be worked into the soil around mature lilacs, although their underskirts are usually too rooty to cultivate easily. If you can't dig the lime in properly, just mix it with aged manure and compost, then ladle the mixture on as a mulch in late fall or early spring. Spread it in an even blanket several inches deep, starting from the base of the stems and extending to a few inches past the drip line of each shrub.

Exceptionally heady fragrance contrasts can be created by partnering lilac with scented peonies and then counterbalancing the sweetness with pungent aromatics like artemisia, lavender, and rosemary.

Hawthorn

The hawthorn may peak any time from mid-May into June, when its quintessentially English scent floods the garden. To those who didn't grow up with hawthorn, it may smell a bit musty and not over-whelmingly nice. For those who did, the scent can be intensely evocative. An English friend who visited recently declared himself to be having a Proustian total-recall experience, thanks to an extravaganza of bloom from an enormous old hawthorn in my garden. Cradling a flower-decked branch in his hand, snuffling it blissfully, he trans-ported both of us to the garden of his childhood, which was bounded at one end by an old hedgerow of hawthorn and elder, with a damp ditch beneath it. Listening to his recollections, I, too, could see the grassy banks thick with wild primroses and violets and celandines. To my knowl-edge, hawthorn is not a controlled substance, but perhaps investigation might reveal it to be more interesting in composition than hitherto suspected.

May tree, or English hawthorn (*Crataegus laevi-gata*, to 25'), is a splendid tree when left to its own natural shape, but too often it is tormented into lollipop lumps that add nothing to the landscape. Unfortunately, several of the most popular forms spend most of their life disfig-ured by various fungal blights, aphid encampments, and leaf spots. Fortunately, at least one very pretty May tree boasts significant resistance to these problems. Hot red

'Crimson Cloud' (also sold as 'Superba') has spangled, white-eyed flowers like bonfire sparks that give way to sumptuous displays of ruddy hips in fall. This makes a much better choice than the usual 'Paul's Scarlet', an older plant that is rarely healthy in the Northwest.

Our native American Washington thorn, *C. phaenopyrum* (to 25'), is one of the very nicest garden hawthorns. In May it carries a generous load of mildly fragrant white flowers, followed in summer by glossy red fruits. The autumn color can be spectacular, though it isn't always, so it's worth selecting young trees in fall, which is also a great time to plant them. In winter, Washington thorn offers a lovely silhouette, the bold, horizontal lines of its branches contrasting handsomely with the lacy, fine-textured twigs.

Pair hawthorn sprigs with primroses and violets for a classic tussie-mussie.

People who want smaller, less thorny trees might consider planting silver hawthorn, *C. laciniata* (to 15'), instead. Compact and shapely, this nearly thornless little tree has clean white, softly scented flowers, followed by fat, tomato red fruits much appreciated by the birds. The small, tidy flowers color nicely in fall, and its rounded head and rugged bark, striped and flaking, are handsome in winter. All the hawthorns benefit from a periodic, judicious thinning of the young shoots that can crowd the inner branches. None, however, will benefit from being hacked about; hard pruning not only stimulates more new growth than ever but also promotes the many diseases that plague hawthorns. A good rule of thumb is not to prune at all, unless a tree has become unsightly. Moderate thinning of interior branches will open up a crowded crown nicely, and should be repeated only occasionally, when strictly necessary.

Wallflowers

By midspring, the wallflowers are in full fig, spilling their generous, spicy perfume throughout the garden. In England, wallflowers, *Erysimum* [*Cheiranthus*], are often planted against a warm, south-facing house wall with a window that can be opened to let the clovelike scent indoors. Among the most fragrant is a robust hybrid called *Erysimum* 'Bowles Mauve' [*Cheiranthus* 'Bowles Mauve'] (to 3'), a shrubby-looking perennial that can become enormously fat in time. Evergreen and almost everblooming, this hard worker often wears itself out in a few years, but it earns itself perpetual replacement in sunny gardens, where it can be incredibly productive. Its slim, grey-green leaves and big, showy spikes of warm mauve blossoms blend nicely with the colors, shapes, and scents of herbs like lavenders, sages, and rosemaries. As experimental gardeners know, there isn't much that 'Bowles Mauve' doesn't complement, and it fits comfortably into nearly any kind of garden scheme.

Perennial bedding wallflowers, *Erysimum cheiri* [*Cheiranthus cheiri*] (to 2'), are smaller versions of 'Bowles Mauve' that offer a range of warm, sunset colors. Their foot-long spires come in hot reds and deep burgundy, tawny oranges and chocolaty browns, old gold and yolk yellows, as well as gentle shades of butter and cream. Wallflowers live longest when they are deadheaded and pruned back hard after blooming, but they are so easy to grow from seed that it's no tragedy when they fly away to plant heaven. Grow the seedlings in a nursery bed, then sort by color before placing them into display beds or borders. Their intense, almost smoky sweetness makes them splendid company for daphnes and early viburnums, but because bedding wallflowers prefer rich soils and plenty of moisture, they are less appropriate partners for

the Mediterraneans that accompany 'Bowles Mauve' so well. The white or rosy ones make a truly memorable underplanting for a wall covered in a violet-scented cascade of climbing Lady Banks roses.

Lady Banks Roses

Lady Banks roses, or Banksian roses, as forms of *Rosa banksiae* (10–20') are called, are deliciously fragrant spring bloomers that thrive in a warm, sunny, sheltered position. These Chinese climbers were named after the wife of the director of England's Kew gardens at the turn of the eighteenth century. Thornless and glossy-leaved, they make very attractive wall coverings near a seating area, but in the cool summer areas of the maritime Northwest, they need the sunniest possible spot if they are to bloom as generously as they can. The white form, *R. b.* var. *normalis*, has the most dazzling scent, which is like ethereal violets that have died and gone to heaven. The flowers are charming rather than magnificent, with papery, ragged-edged petals centered with a tiny boss that is rosy pink in newly opened flowers but turns pale gold as the blossoms mature. A delicate golden fringe of stamens makes the flowers glow softly, as if they were candlelit from within. Rose books are always saying that the yellow forms of *R. banksiae* don't have any scent, but they definitely do, although it is not as intense as in the white form. Any Banksian rose will make a memorable companion for anemone clematis (*Clematis montana*), for their scents are as compatible as their tender colorations.

More Early Roses

Here in the Northwest, roses can throw a bloom or two in nearly any month of the year. However, a handful are both exception-

ally fragrant and reliably early, spangling the borders with their bright blossoms in April and May. One of my favorites is the seldom-grown incense rose, *Rosa primula* (to 6'), a dainty shrub that gets broader rather than higher with age. The glossy, fine-textured leaves smell powerfully of incense (the nice Japanese kind, not the smelly paraphernalia shop kind). This effect is most pronounced on warm, still days, when the delicate, wild-rose scent of the flowers is also at its strongest. The best specimen I ever saw was planted in a crack between a sunny wall and the sidewalk in the Seattle garden of the late Kevin Nicolay, eminent gardener and botanical artist extraordinaire. In colder gardens, this heat lover may sulk, producing very few of its golden flowers.

Similar in looks but much easier to please is *Rosa* 'Canary Bird' (to 8'), a bushy shrub rose that is airy enough in construction to fit comfortably into the smallest gardens. The slim stems are decked in April and May with single, pale yellow roses the size of an old silver dollar. This year, Kate Gessert, a garden writer from Eugene, Oregon, demanded to know what was wafting that delicious smell of freesias through my garden. We traced it to this rose, which has a complex floral fragrance very similar to that of freesias. By late afternoon, as she was leaving, she came running back to announce that now the rose smelled like sweet peas, which combine the confectionery scents of orange blossom and vanilla.

Star Magnolia

A curving, multitrunked star magnolia, *Magnolia stellata* (to 12'), is another excellent thing to plant near a Banksian rose. Graceful in branch and long-fingered in twig, star magnolia tends to have a lot of character even when youthful. It also blooms generously from an early age, opening silky, loose-petaled flowers from plump, fuzzy buds in early spring. The

shrub itself is quite hardy, but the buds can be damaged by sudden low temperatures. Plant it where it gets plenty of sun, but avoid an eastern exposure, for frozen buds that thaw slowly usually bloom undamaged, while those hit by early-morning light in winter generally explode instead. A solid or evergreen windbreak to the east will also provide helpful protection from bitter winds, which can blacken the first buds despite their furry jackets.

At least half a dozen forms of star magnolia are widely available, with white, pink, or rosy flowers that may be single or double. All are especially wonderful choices for smaller gardens where the big magnolias would be too much of a good thing. All are also fabulously fragrant, with a slightly lemony tang that cuts the rather cloying sweetness of the familial perfume. This is a lovely shrub to plant beneath a bedroom window or by the front entry, where it can be appreciated daily. In one of my favorite gardens, an elegantly twisted star magnolia is backed by an arching fountain of Buffalo currant, which pours out its spicy scent from April through May.

Buffalo Currant

Buffalo currant, *Ribes odoratum* (5–8'), is a deciduous shrub native to the Midwest. Well-grown plants form spreading mounds, twiggy and airily trimmed in small, multilobed leaves and remaining decently clad clear to the ground. Unhappy ones can be ungainly and so leggy that the powerfully scented flowers can't quite earn them garden space. The secret is to give them full sun and decent but not overly rich soil. Don't waste the best places on these cheerful creatures—save those for roses or bearded iris. Currants would rather be lined along a hot driveway than live the fat life in the border. In such a spot, they will produce quantities of tiny, tubular yellow flowers that smell powerfully of cloves and carnations. The yellow is a fresh, clear color that looks

good with almost anything. As they mature, however, they turn a very handsome coppery orange that swears horribly with pinkish bricks, as friends of mine discovered. Fruiting types like 'Crandall' offer a bonus of glossy black berries that make very tasty currant jelly. Be sparing with the water in summer, or the fruits will be flaccid and bland. (However, the bushes will be more productive when kept adequately moist in dry years.)

Golden currant, *R. aureum* (to 10'), a Northwestern native, is quite similar looking, and the best forms have a similarly sparkling, spicy fragrance. Seedlings are variable in this regard, so wait till spring and give the candidates the sniff test to be sure you're getting a yummy one. They are also variable as to fruit color and quality; the berries of golden currant can be yellow, red, or black, and only the black ones are worth eating. This complicates the selection process, and since the plants actually prefer to live east of the mountains, buffalo currant is probably a better choice.

Buffalo currant is not the best garden mixer, so grow it by the sidewalk or driveway, where it can bask in reflected heat. ❧

Sweet Violet

I grow a number of sweet violets, *Viola odorata* (to 4"), tucked underneath my buffalo currants. Although they sow themselves and grow beautifully all over the garden, those in the leanest, sunniest conditions are not only the first to bloom but also have the strongest scent. Indeed, violets growing in richer, moister soils tend to make far more leaves than flowers. Perhaps because in nature, violets appreciate ordinary woodsy conditions, they perform better in the garden when under a little stress. This doesn't mean we can neglect or mistreat them, but we can expect them to thrive in dry, even rather rooty places, along hedges, or

under mature trees and shrubs. The first violets often appear in late winter, but by March, most clumps will be solidly purple with exceptionally fragrant bloom.

Primrose

rimroses of all kinds thrive in the moderate Northwestern climate, especially the sweet-faced bedders called polyanthus or *Primula polyantha*. Many of them are nicely fragrant, particularly those with white or yellow flowers. The blues and reds are practically always scentless, though, so here too it's wise to sniff out your favorites when you shop. Several other primrose species smell very pleasing, notably cowslips, *Primula veris* (to 8"). These have leaves like a baby cos ("Romaine") lettuce and dangling yellow flowers in soft bunches with a mild and innocent fragrance. Tall-stemmed *P. florindae* (to 3') are very strongly scented, spilling a pervasive, spice-cookie perfume from large bunches of yellow, golden, or biscuit-colored bells in July. These like shade and damp feet, making them naturals for a streamside position, but they also do well in any deep soil that has plenty of humus to retain adequate moisture. The big, violet-blue spikes of *P. vialii* (to 2') look like little red-hot-poker plants, and offer a complex, floral scent that is especially strong in newly opened florets. These fascinating summer-blooming primroses prefer sunnier though still moist situations, where they may seed themselves modestly. This is good, since they don't live very long in these parts. They are very easy to grow from seed, so just save a seedpod or two and sow them in pots to be sure of a steady supply.

Rockcress

ike primroses, old-fashioned wall rockcress, *Arabis caucasica* (6"), is nearly always grown in company with leathery bergenia and basket of

gold (*Aurinia saxatile*). It makes an attractive, evergreen ground cover for sunny, well-drained banks or rock walls, particularly where its fragrance can be appreciated close at hand. Some people insist that rockcress smells like almonds, but to me, the single-flowered form smells like warm cherry pie, while the double one smells like Danish pastry. In either case, the greyish, slightly furry leaves set off its own clean white flowers in spring and make a handsome backdrop for serial displays of bulbs and perennials all through the year. If you have a carpet of rockcress already (as so many of us do), try interspersing some violet-scented *Iris reticulata* (a spring bloomer), and winter-flowering, grape-juice-scented *Iris unguicularis* with a few lemon-scented spikes of *Chlidanthus fragrans* and a few late-flowering milk-and-wine lilies (*Crinum bulbispermum*) for a full year of perfume.

Not all rockcress is fragrant, but those that are weave lovely, tweedy, heather-flecked blankets over a sunny, dry bank. ∾

California rockcress, *Arabis blepharophylla* (to 8"), is a striking native with sage green leaves and rose-burgundy blossoms that have a strong and carrying floral fragrance only a bit softer than that of hyacinths. A clump former rather than a sprawling mat, this one needs quick drainage and plenty of sun to thrive. It does beautifully in the cracks of a wall or between pavers on a sunny terrace and makes a good partner for aromatic Mediterranean subshrubs like lavender and rosemary.

Lily of the Valley

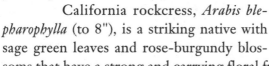

The chubby bells of lily of the valley always remind me of fat, fluted little cups from a child's tea set. To other eyes, they suggest ivory chalices, waxen blueberry flowers, or, in the words of the old song, "White coral bells upon a slender stalk." Whatever they

look like, everybody agrees that they smell exactly like themselves. The delectable fragrance is beloved wherever these hardy bulbs are grown; in one Seattle shop, I found beautiful bars of superfatted French soap scented with *muguet des bois*, Italian bath cream *al mughetto*, and Swiss hand lotion *mit Maiglockchen*, as well as lily of the valley eau de toilette, bath crystals, perfume, and essential oils from all over the world.

Happily for those of us who love its fragrance, nothing could be easier to grow than lily of the valley, *Convallaria majalis* (to 8"). Give them a shady spot in any good garden soil, enrich it with an annual mulch of compost and aged manure, and the plump little pips (bulblets) will reward your efforts with a steadily increasing supply of flowers in April and May. If older plantings taper off their production, they are probably overcrowded. It's a lot of work to dig up a whole bed of these willing workers, so just remove about a third of the plants every few years. Take them out in 6- to 8-inch plugs, replacing them with more compost and manure. The holes will fill in quickly, and all the plants will bloom better for the thinning. Start new colonies in other parts of the garden with the extras, or pass them on to friends with new gardens, who will be very pleased to have them.

Exit Spring, Enter Summer

Mid-May is usually fairly quiet in terms of flowers. Indeed, for most foliage fanciers, this is the favorite time of year. So many leafy plants are at their peak of perfection just now that the relative dearth of flowers does not mar the garden one whit. This isn't to say that there's nothing doing, only that graceful, nodding columbines, citrus-colored Welsh poppies, and tall late tulips often provide most of mid-May's floral display.

In warm years, however, the typical, protracted Northwestern spring is accelerated by the sudden heat. Before we know it, the apple blossom has vanished from the trees, and the pale pink, fragrant petal snow that litters the grass has turned brown. One fine sunny day, we suddenly realize that those proud tulips are decidedly worse for wear. The columbines and Welsh poppies will carry on for quite a while, but they no longer take the eye as they did without competition. All those modest late-spring bloomers are hustled off-stage early by the arrival of bolder, showier beauties as spring slips into summer.

One May dazzler that can hold a candle to anything summer offers is the beautybush, *Kolkwitzia amabilis* (8–12'). Brought to this country at the turn of the century by Ernest 'Chinese' Wilson, beautybush was very much a collector's plant until the 1920s, when it was popularized by Jackson & Perkins Nursery (now best known as rose specialists). This graceful shrub then became so ubiquitous that it fell from favor, shunned as old-fashioned and common. Now it is rarely seen outside of older gardens, which is a pity since it is a very deserving, multiseasonal shrub. Mature plants are vase-shaped with slim waists and arching branches that pour down a fragrant cascade of rosy or chalky pink. The fluted, tubular flowers have furry white throats faintly freckled with gold. Their wonderful scent, honeyed and slightly fruity, is especially magical on warm evenings, when it wanders freely through the garden, and again at petalfall, when the lawn is thick with sweet flowers after a windy night.

Beautybush has a soft, velvety scent that combines deliciously with roses. ❧

As the blossoms mature, the swelling seedpods beneath them become covered with fluffy white fur that always reminds me of a rabbitskin muff I coveted as a girl. As the seed heads ripen, they become quite large and quietly attractive, turning a lovely, rusty cinnamon color,

with a light, frizzy texture. These remain handsome well into autumn, when the foliage turns gentle coppers and muted reds. In winter, the exfoliating bark can be seen, hanging from the slim trunks in long, papery strips like greyish brown raffia.

Beautybush will grow well in any decent garden soil, but prefers drier rather than damp situations. It flowers most heavily in full sun, and shrubs grown in open, sunny sites will be shapelier than those in shade. Where older plants have grown leggy and graceless or shy blooming, prune back the oldest branches to promote new growth. Very young plants should be trimmed of seed heads to reduce stress (it takes energy to make seeds) and to encourage bushiness. Flopsy plants can be staked with rebar until the woody framework ripens sufficiently to stand up nicely on its own.

In my garden, a huge, rosy old beautybush called 'Pink Cloud' makes a spectacular backdrop shrub for a deep border outside my kitchen window. By late May, the shrub is in its glory, its warm color strengthened by sprays of ruddier 'Betty Prior' roses that have scrambled through the lower branches. This rose is supposed to be a five-footer, but this one had been goat-pruned for many years and had developed climbing tendencies in self-defense. The flowers are lovely together, as are their mingled scents.

At month's end, the first plum tart iris, *Iris graminea* (to 18"), are thrusting thready, grey-blue blossoms through the grassy foliage. The slim little flowers are richly plum-scented, though there is some debate as to whether the fruits in question are plums or apricots and whether they are fresh or stewed. To my nose, the curious scent suggests prune plums baked with a touch of 4711 eau de toilette. In any case, these delicious flowers signal the end of spring and the beginning of true summer, regardless of the actual date on which they open. From the time they do, the floral floodgates are opened and the rush of summer is upon us.

Chapter
Three

SUMMER
FRAGRANCES

June, July, August

The roses spill their sweetness, their wandering perfumes offset by piquant bursts of rosemary and lavender, soothing lemon balm and astringent artemisia. ❧

Garden strolls take on a whole new dimension in June, when so many fragrant plants are reaching their peak. Early in the morning, before the sun rouses the roses, the garden is saturated with the deliciously green smell of strongly growing grass. As the day warms up, half a hundred other plants add their individual scents to the air. Touched by sun, the roses spill their sweetness, their wandering perfumes offset by piquant bursts of rosemary and lavender, soothing lemon balm and astringent artemisia. At night, the ebbing, flowing breath of June is rich with jasmine, dark with flowering tobacco, bright with lilies. Many of these scents remain with us for months, intensifying as summer matures.

June brings too many scents to count, but an outstanding few irresistibly demand our attention. Chief among these are roses, whose combined fragrances characterize the beginning of summer. Sweet peas, too, have an ineffable perfume, at once romantic and innocent. I was fascinated to learn that commercial perfumers can nearly duplicate this scent by mixing the essences of vanilla and orange blossom. While true vanilla scent is rare in the garden, the lilting fragrance of orange blossom is rich on the air in June, when sweet mock oranges (*Philadelphus* spp.) and Mexican mock orange (*Choisya ternata*) are in flower together. Unlike real oranges, both of these shrubs grow readily in Northwestern gardens.

The most potent perfumes are often overwhelming up close; yet cleverly placed, they may reward the neighborhood as well as the gardener. Honey-scented black locust trees (*Robinia pseudoacacia*), with their droop-

ing panicles of creamy, pealike blossoms, are too brittle of branch and aggressive of root for small gardens. However, they can transform a funky alley into a Persian love bower when they bloom above the trash cans, perfuming the air for several blocks around in May and June. That blissfully sweet mock orange that grew in Granny's garden (probably *Philadelphus coronarius*) may be too large and shapeless a shrub for a tiny garden, yet tucked away beside the compost bin, it will still fill the garden—indeed, the neighborhood—with its bridal fragrance.

Perhaps the most successful way to marry summer scents is to use the showboat fragrance plants sparingly, relying most heavily on plants with scents that have to be sought out. A great host of foliage plants are rather reserved, releasing little or none of their fragrance on the air until the leaves are handled. Scented geraniums, fruit sage (*Salvia dorisiana*), mints, and many other culinary herbs must be brushed or even crushed to set their lovely smells free. However, flowers, too can be close with their scent; many border perennials smell quite pleasant when you bend over to inspect them closely but are not detectably fragrant until you do so.

Only a handful of plants are completely without scent, but equally few have carrying perfumes that call to us clear across the garden. One of my favorites, mignonette (*Reseda odora*), has crumpled green and beige flowers that look almost ugly. Indeed, their powerful fragrance is so seductively alluring that many people resist making the connection. That heavenly smell could not possibly come from those homely flowers! Similarly, climbing *Rosa soulieana* has sprays of modest, white, single flowers that look too small and simple to produce their incredibly potent perfume.

In Empress

Josephine's day,

the window boxes

of Paris were

filled with the

foamy green and

beige blossoms of

mignonette. ☙

Lingering, nostalgic, and astonishingly sweet, their scent makes up the thrumming base of my garden's perfume from late June into July.

Certain assertive scents need to oxidize, or combine with air, in order to fully develop. At close range, the little pink frizzles of another climbing rose, 'Paul's Himalayan Musk', have a gentle, sweet smell that expands across the garden into a sumptuous scent that knocks your socks off. The small yellow trumpets of evergreen Carolina jessamine, *Gelsemium sempervirens*, have a tender, wistful smell close up; as it blends with sun-warmed air, it strengthens into a singing, sonorous scent that teases the nose by vanishing and reappearing repeatedly when you try to track it to its source.

No matter what kind of fragrance effects you want to orchestrate, there is no better time of year to experiment than in June, when so many insinuating, penetrating, traveling scents are at your disposal. Entertain yourself by varying your arrangements, using pots and containers to keep the plants mobile while you make up your mind about how you want to experience them. It's good to be both playful and patient as you run your trials. Give each idea time to settle in and ripen, for sequences that disappoint by day may delight by night. Be forewarned, however, that an initial flyer into the world of fragrance may well develop into a full-blown passion. Once you have opened yourself fully to your senses by truly paying attention to what *is*, neither you nor your garden will ever be the same.

Fabulously Fragrant Roses

Roses deserve the zillions of books of their own that litter the market, and I'm not even going to try to catalog them for you. What I will do is mention the best-behaved and most fragrant roses in

my own garden. Among the first and finest is 'New Dawn', a prolific climber that is absolutely smothered in perfect, shell pink blossoms for over a month in early summer. These have a delicately delicious fragrance that persists pleasantly in the dried petals, making 'New Dawn' a potpourri favorite. This rose is my idea of a trouper, for it grows happily in heavy clay soil, tolerating our usual summer drought with aplomb, and its glossy foliage never shows a trace of black spot or powdery mildew. What's more, this sturdy independent rarely needs more pruning than what it gets in blossom time, when it provides hundreds of flowers for the house.

Dried rosebuds hold their scent longest if picked in the morning as soon as the dew is dry.

A clambering Chinese species, *Rosa soulieana*, is similarly tough and productive, filling an old pear tree with its lacy foliage and spilling in a creamy curtain from June into July. The little white single roses come in loose clusters, sending forth a rich, fruity scent with fresh, high floral overtones that keep it endlessly satisfying. Indeed, by late June, it is almost drinkable, and pervades the entire garden morning and night. The flowers are followed by tiny red hips that feed birds all winter, giving this lusty plant several seasons of beauty. It needs very little pruning, which is just as well, since its small thorns are generously distributed and cruelly adherent.

The new English (or David Austin) roses deserve special mention for beauty, excellent health, and outstanding fragrance. My absolute favorite is 'Windrush' (6–8'), a semidouble rose with large, matte green leaves and a relatively handsome bush shape. (Few roses are genuinely shapely.) 'Windrush' opens from warm yellow buds into creamy white blossoms with buttery hearts. Their scent is buttery as well, rich and warm with a smooth,

lingering finish. This one blooms in flushes from June into autumn, when its plump, ruddy hips bend the slim stems to the ground.

Other exceptional performers include two compact border shrub roses, the peachy-salmon 'Nymphenburg' (to 6'), whose sugary scent combines new-mown grass with green apples, and little 'Nathalie Nypels' (to 3'), a polyantha/floribunda hybrid whose loose sprays of ruffly, pale pink flowers have a fine and flowery fragrance. Nothing ever mars the foliage of these two hard workers, both of which bloom repeatedly well into autumn.

No fragrance garden is complete without a plant of a German hybrid called 'Fragrant Cloud' (also sold as 'Duftwolke'). Hot red buds open into smoky, salmon red blossoms that admittedly lack subtlety. However, they offer an exceptional perfume, intense enough to evoke the "Wow!" reflex in most visitors. So, too, does my all-time favorite tea rose, 'Just Joey'. Dazzling confections in apricot, ginger, and peach, the huge blossoms teeter on the edge of vulgarity, like those hats beloved of the Royal Family. Their smell is as sumptuous as their coloration, and they provide as much pleasure to the border colorist as to the organizer of garden perfumes.

Old-fashioned eglantine (*Rosa rubiginosa*, to 8') is often called the sweet briar rose for its outstanding scent. In midsummer, this very prickly, upright plant is covered with single, baby pink roses with a very pretty wild-rose scent. When the flowers pass, they are replaced by shining masses of dark red hips that remain attractive well into winter. However, the real glory of this vigorous shrub is its foliage, which is finely textured with a matte finish and utterly permeated with a deliciously aromatic, spicy fragrance that rivals that of any rose. This scent is not always obvious unless one crushes a leaf, but at certain times it will fill the garden of its own accord. Warm, wet winds like our spring chinook always awaken the leaf perfume, which is also very strong after summer rains. In old English gardens, a sweet briar is often found at the southwest corner of the garden, where the foliar perfume will be carried through the garden to the house after warm summer rains.

Pineapple Broom

Another wonderful, wandering fragrance belongs to pineapple broom (*Cytisus battandieri*, to 15'), a beautiful, undemanding plant with multiple beauties over a long season. Few people would readily identify it as a broom, for its fat, straw yellow flower spikes look more like lupines than like ordinary Scotch broom, and the grey, trifoliate leaves, silky with silver fur, look rather like velveteen clover. This biggest of the garden brooms (which, indeed, is sometimes called Atlas broom) is a wonderful shrub for a protected, south-facing wall, where it will remain decently clothed all winter through most of its range. (Even in Seattle, it is reliably evergreen in most years.) Each spring, it drops its tarnished pewter leaves for brand-new ones, which emerge sage green hazed with fine white hairs.

June brings on the plump blossoms, which continue in bursts into autumn. The warm yellow florets are packed in bunches that so recall the shape of a pineapple, it's no wonder our noses are prepared to smell that fruit when we sniff them. In fact, these flowers offer a fruit-punch scent, combining not just pineapple but tangerine and mandarin orange, with a touch of kumquat and a trace of lime.

I don't know why this plant is so seldom grown, for it is not very hard to please. Ordinary, well-drained garden soil

The flowers of pineapple sage offer a fruit punch scent.

∾

and plenty of sun keep pineapple broom happy for years. Given a south-facing wall to reflect sun and heat, the older stems will ripen nicely, producing quantities of blossom after a sunny summer. Protection from bitter winter winds will reduce winter dieback, but even after a hard year, there will be ample flowers to brighten the air. A large and silvery *Artemisia*, perhaps the lusty 'Huntington's Variety' or 'Powis Castle', will complement this big beauty in both color and scent, providing a refreshingly astringent, herbal fragrance to balance the intense sweetness of the broom blossom.

Fragrant Clouds of Clematis

One of my favorite scented plants is a bush clematis, *Clematis recta*, which is a perennial rather than a climber. The name *recta* means upright, which the plants are for the early part of the season, forming a shrubby clump as much as seven feet tall (most often they range from three to four feet). However, the minute the blossom begins to open, the entire plant slumps over, smothering anything in its wake beneath its scented bosom. Perhaps those busy botanists could rename this one *C. prostrata*, for this flopsy habit is most distressing to the unprepared gardener. Happily, there are several excellent ways to cope. One is not to plant anything you like around the clematis. This has the merit of simplicity, but isn't lastingly satisfactory. You can also plant bush clematis on top of a wall or a bank where it can cascade without harm. It looks staggeringly lovely in such a position, creating a fragrant, creamy cloud of blossom. However, such places are generally quite dry, and because clematis hate dry roots, it's vital to provide them with wonderful, deep, rich soil and plenty of moisture. A handful of a hydrated hydrophilic polymer such as Broadleaf P4 will also help keep a clematis happy by providing little reservoirs for the roots.

My own preferred coping method is to give each plant a large, four-tiered tomato cage in early May, winding weeping willow wands around the metal frame to reduce its shiny obtrusiveness. If it's early summer and you have only just learned about this slumping habit, there is still time for a modified version of the cage; cut away the hind third of one or two three-tiered cages (each functioning piece will have two rather than three legs), and then support the reclining clematis with them. (Have a friend help by holding the swooning plant while you shove the cage legs in the ground.)

Perhaps this sounds like a lot of trouble; it isn't, really—or needn't be. Like so many chores, this staking takes perhaps three minutes if done early, but requires ten times that if done a little too late. Anyway, *C. recta* is definitely worth a bit of trouble, for it persists in billowing blossom for over a month, often reblooming sporadically through the summer. A happy bush clematis can produce galaxies of starry little flowers the color of moonlight. On a warm June day (should there be such a thing), their wild, sweet scent carries nicely across the garden, but on cool, wet, windy days, you have to bury your face in the flowers to discover their full potential.

A blue-belled cousin, *C. heracleifolia* (to 4'), is equally fragrant. Generally treated as a perennial, this sturdy bush clematis is less floppy than *C. recta*, holding its tight, globular clusters of ice-blue bell flowers above large, trilobed leaves. In midsummer, the blossoms send out a distinctive and delicious scent that combines ripe plums with lemon and honey. Golden lemon balm, *Melissa* 'Allgold', makes a pretty and pungent companion, moderating the sweetness with a pleasingly citric tang.

Where ground space is limited, consider draping walls and fences with fragrant climbing clematis. Many species smell wonderful, including the primrose-scented *C. rehderiana* (10–25'), a delicate, ferny-leaved scrambler with fragrant, chalk yellow bells, and *C. serratifolia*, a more

robust creature with appropriately serrate leaves and larger, lemon yellow bells with the rich, warm scent of lemon curd.

Chocolate Cosmos

There is a purple-leaved form of bush clematis called *Clematis recta* 'Purpurea', which smells just as good as the plain one. In my garden, this dark beauty is underplanted with chocolate cosmos, *Cosmos atrosanguineus* (2'). This fitful perennial has coarser foliage than its annual cousin cosmos, and its mahogany red flowers look like single dahlias (which are also close kin). Their scrumptious smell puts them in a league of their own, for they are redolent of hot chocolate, bittersweet and milky.

These curious plants form fat storage roots much as dahlias do, and they need the same kind of treatment. Give them full sun and rich, deep soil, and you will enjoy the deep red flowers from midsummer into autumn. A thick mulch will keep them warm enough to winter over most years, but you can dig up a root or two to store (again, just as with dahlias) if you want to be sure of keeping this delightful plant. The foliage emerges quite late in spring, and is fatally attractive to slugs, so a circle of diatomaceous earth will help ensure its safe arrival above ground. Once well up, the plants seem able to defend themselves, blooming staunchly all summer without further damage.

Mock Oranges

The traditional mock orange found in every New England yard, *Philadelphus coronarius*, produces one of the most powerful and carrying scents in the garden. Indeed, a row of elderly plants at a neighbor's can be smelled a tenth of a mile away—like my sons' gym

socks, but far, far nicer. The sensitive may find its olfactory excesses unbearable, but most of us revel in them, delighting in such unstinting generosity. *P. coronarius* makes a big plant (to 12'), if not an especially lovely one, and older bushes can look quite untidy. To restore shape, prune them hard after blooming (or during, if you like that staggering scent in the house, as I do), removing older stems to make room for younger growth.

The best way

to buy mock orange

is to visit nurseries

in June. ᴄ⍵

Smaller mock oranges abound, with scents varied both in kind and in quantity. Give them the sniff test before you buy, for some are actually scentless (these were bred for cold-hardiness, not fragrance). An older hybrid, 'Virginal' (8'), offers loosely doubled white blossoms with a sumptuous scent, while midsized 'Avalanche' (5') has larger, single flowers with a lighter, fruitier fragrance. For the smallest gardens, there's baby *P. microphyllus* (3'), a compact, fine-textured shrub that provides weeks of potently perfumed, single white flowers in May and June.

Mexican mock orange, *Choisya ternata* (6–8'), is a glossy, densely furnished evergreen shrub with three-fingered foliage and loose clusters of starry white flowers that both look and smell like orange blossom. In milder regions, it begins blooming in late winter, continuing through spring into summer. Although the blossom quantity tapers as summer deepens, a few sprays are always open for the pleasure of bees and wandering gardeners. Pick all the flowers you like, because this plant needs a lot of thinning to keep it shapely. Not surprisingly, mock orange mingles deliciously with most roses. For an outrageous floral explosion, thread a honeysuckle up a nearby tree in the neighborhood of your mock orange. The result is almost overpowering at close range, but hauntingly romantic at a distance, particularly at night.

Honeysuckle

lthough honeysuckles are discussed more fully in Chapter Six, "Night-Fragrant Plants," they deserve a mention here as well, for these powerfully fragrant plants play a major role in many summer perfumes. Silky, insinuating, and subtle, the scent of honeysuckle is among summer's nicest treats. Changeling in nature, it alters through the day, being sweetly floral in morning, faint and spicy by day, then aromatic and fruity by night. Strongest and most carrying early and late, honeysuckle perfume seems designed to delight the working stiff who is rarely able to enjoy the midday garden. In fact, this most generous of scents is oddly shy in the heat of the day, when one has to bury one's nose in a cluster of blossom to experience what is poured out with abandon from afternoon till morning.

Unimproved roses used as root stock for named roses often smell better than the neon-bright hybrids they support. ❧

Perhaps the most commonly grown is that rampant climber, Hall's honeysuckle (*L. japonica* 'Halliana'). This lusty creature first twines itself upward to a height of perhaps fifteen feet. Not content with the high life, it then spreads itself widely, covering as much as a hundred and fifty feet of wall or wood or whatever happens to be in its path. Not a plant for a small garden, it is a delightful one all the same, spilling its superb scent from large clusters of frilly cream and gold flowers all summer long.

In my present garden, Hall's honeysuckle had announced itself to my nose long before it was revealed to the eye by a swinging machete. The enormous old plant had twisted itself around a companionable climbing rose—a sweet old thing with fragrant, crumpled flowers like puffs of pale pink tissue. Twined tightly together, they filled the arms of an elderly apple tree. By night, their

combined scents make a wandering, winsome perfume that recalls the old Lee Wiley number called "Honeysuckle Rose," in which she sings of love far sweeter than sugar. This perfume is like that: sweet yet spicy, soft yet penetrating. It arrives in pulses on the warm evening air, now stronger, now fainter, retreating with the breeze, bolstered by a drop in temperature. After a day of heavy rain, the scent rolls in like fog, luring me out to the garden bench to watch the moon wheel across the luminous night sky.

Where space is limited, many another deliciously scented honeysuckle could contribute its fragrance. *Lonicera* × *americana* (to 20') is a handsome climber with an astonishingly potent, spicy scent spilling from soft, salmony pink and sherbet orange blossoms. Both fine-textured box honeysuckle, *L. nitida* (to 6'), and the dapper little privet honeysuckle, *L. pileata*, have fragrant white flowers with a soft, fruity sweetness, the former in June, the latter in May. Nicest of all is the lilac honeysuckle, *L. syringantha* (to 6'). Compact in form and bitty of leaf, this border shrub carries masses of tiny lavender florets with a high, heady floral scent that mingles especially well with brisk lavender and gentle, insinuating mignonette.

Jasmine

On my most memorable trip to California's Bay Area, I stayed in a small hotel where several flights of stairs led to cabins perched high over the water. The climb was eased by walls smothered in jasmine and underplanted with gardenias, their scents combining in an unforgettable living perfume. In English cottage gardens, jasmine was traditionally planted along the garden path that led, rather less romantically, to the outhouse. (To this day, when we talk of leading somebody up the garden path, we imply that they will be getting a nasty, rather than a nice, surprise.) The delicious smell of

the flowers was meant to offset the less-acceptable ones emanating from the family privy.

Fortunately, jasmine has less-prosaic connotations these days, and we can enjoy its supernal scent without that earthy counterpoint. In the Pacific Northwest, we can grow quite a number of species and hybrids, enjoying them from midspring in warmer areas all through the summer and well into fall. Spanish jasmine, *Jasminum grandiflorum* (12–15'), has enormous, clean white blossoms, and is a bit hardier than poet's jasmine, *J. officinale* (to 20'), which produces quantities of smaller but still intensely fragrant white flowers. Both are evergreen in mild years, semideciduous in cold ones. Rosy, long-necked *J. × stephanense* (to 8') looks delicate but is tougher than either one. This shaggy scrambler makes a better choice in colder gardens, even though it produces smaller and less abundant flowers than its lusty cousins. Where sun and warmth are plentiful, no vine is more ardent in bloom than *J. polyanthum* (to 20'). This is the lacy creeper sold in hanging baskets to brighten the house in winter (which it does very well indeed). Release it from its basket and let it pour through a large fruit tree, perhaps in company with a climbing rose like silvery mauve 'Climbing Angel Face', itself no slouch in the scent department.

Whichever you choose, your jasmine will be most productive and suffer the least winter damage when given a sheltered, sunny position. All prefer garden soils that are retentive of moisture and well enriched with aged manure and compost. Though jasmines aren't terribly picky about pH, they perform better in very acid soils when those are buffered with plenty of compost (which is usually pH-neutral). It is also helpful to mix a handful of dolomite lime into their mulch each spring and fall. (See

Encourage hardy jasmine to clamber over a sheltered porch where it gets plenty of sun. ❧

also Chapter Six, "Night-Fragrant Plants.") Jasmine needs no help to smell sumptuous, but when it is planted near mock orange, the two scents mingle with intoxicating results. Jasmines also combine delightfully with most roses. Don't try to mix in lilies, through, or the effect becomes unpleasantly cloying, with a curiously rank finish.

Lilies

No fragrant garden is complete without lilies, for they provide some of the most compelling, insistent notes in the high summer perfume. Not all are scented, but those that are often have more than their fair share of potency. Among the best are regal and madonna lilies, the towering trumpets and Oriental hybrids, and Chinese gold band lilies. A handful of lesser-known species, including Northwestern natives like checkered *Lilium kelloggii* and lemony *L. parryi*, are similarly gifted. However, since they are not easy to grow well (or indeed, at all), these natives should be enjoyed in the wild, letting their lusty kin take pride of place in the garden.

Greatest of garden performers, the regal lily, *L. regale* (3–4') tolerates heavy, acid clay soils and blooms as well in light shade as in full sun. Its long, purple-stained buds open into glowing white goblets spilling with golden pollen that stains your nose for days if you drink too deeply of its intoxicating scent. Regal lilies

come quickly from seed, reaching blooming size in just two or three years, so it's easy to have plenty of them around. They look wonderful nestled beneath red-leaved *Rosa rubrifolia* or poking up between a fragrant black bugbane, *Cimicifuga ramosa* 'Atropurpurea', and ruddy St. John's wort, *Hypericum androsaemum* 'Albury Purple'.

MADONNA LILIES

Madonna lilies grow best in company, so partner them with apricot foxgloves, peachy roses, and clouds of seakale.

For centuries, madonna lilies, *Lilium candidum* (to 5'), have decorated gardens throughout the western world. Demure and elegant, their sleek white trumpets send out a caressing fragrance that deepens mysteriously by night. When they are planted near honeysuckle, the two scents combine in a silky, delightfully complex perfume. Unlike most lilies, madonna lilies require shallow planting; their tips should rest just below the soil surface, and they should never be smothered by mulch. Their tufty new growth appears in early autumn, remaining evergreen all winter. Resist the impulse to give them a warm winter blanket of leaves or straw, for these resting rosettes need plenty of light and air. Madonna lilies smell really lovely when grown near lightly scented roses like 'Nathalie Nypels' or 'New Dawn', and clove-and-nutmeg-scented wallflowers.

TRUMPET LILIES

Robust trumpet lilies are complex hybrids with multiple parents, so seed-grown plants may vary a good deal, both from the seed parent and from each other. Named clones, such as the famous 'Black Dragon' trumpet lily, should all be identical to the original plant. When you buy a supposedly black dragon that turns out ruby or purple or green, is only three feet tall instead of six, or has

only a few, not especially fragrant, flowers, you got a seedling, not a true clone. Don't patronize that plant source again (do write and tell them why you won't), but seek out more reliable suppliers. Luckily for us, the Pacific Northwest has a number of excellent growers whose plants are true to name, healthy, and generously sized. Expect to pay more for plants of this quality, knowing that a lot of work goes into producing them. In this case, it's worth paying more to get what you really want.

Among my personal favorite trumpets are the greenish ones like the 'Moonlight' strain, which runs from pale chartreuse through butter and creamy gold. Their soft, intensely sweet smell is lightened by a touch of lemon, making them splendid companions for richly scented roses. The Olympic hybrids come in a delicious blend of sherbet colors, raspberry and peach, apricot and banana—one of the few mixtures that really is uniformly lovely. More expensive named forms like 'Green Magic' and 'Quicksilver' are best for artful border schemes where uniformity of color and size is important. All offer equally strong contrasts of form and fragrance to rounded, spice-scented garden companions like butterfly bushes (*Buddleia*) and phlox.

Stem-rooting trumpet lilies appreciate humus-rich but well-drained soils and plenty of light. The flowers last longer in color and scent when grown in light or dappled shade, though most tolerate morning sun quite well. Deep planting and a thick mulch will conserve the moisture lilies crave and will moderate soil temperatures in hot weather.

Gold Band and Oriental Hybrid Lilies

Chinese gold band lilies (*Lilium auratum*, to 6'), grow better in the Pacific Northwest than anywhere else in the country, but they can still be finicky, especially in heavy soils. Still, they are well worth pleasing, because few flowers look or smell as flat-out gorgeous as these

huge, curling white lilies, delicately freckled in cinnamon and striped with palest gold. Their offspring, the late-blooming Oriental hybrid lilies (to 3'), are rather easier to please and offer a delicious variety of coloration, being stippled and striped in pale or rosy pink. In some, the usual pattern is reversed, so pink petals are striped with gold or silver.

Like the parent species, Oriental hybrids flower in late summer, often continuing into autumn. Variable in form, the flowers may be large, cupped goblets, as in 'Magic Pink'; flat-faced beauties with wind-tossed curls such as 'Imperial Silver'; or wide, almost starry flowers, like the popular, raspberry-jam-colored 'Journey's End'. Gleaming white 'Casa Blanca' dangles enormous flowers like silken starfish from sturdy, four-foot stems. Even larger 'Imperial Crimson' is a floral valentine, its heart's-blood-red petals spangled with silvery stardust. Partner any of them with lavender and yarrow (*Achillea*) to create a truly delicious perfume.

Lilies only thrive in well-drained but rich soils. ❦

Northwestern gardeners with loamy, sand-based soils usually enjoy prolonged success with lilies. In such gardens, many lilies will multiply rather than dwindle, as they do where winter rains turn clay soils into waterlogged quagmires. Those who garden on clay will have better luck with lilies if they plant them deeply (dig holes at least a foot deep). Before setting the bulbs, drop in three or four inches of grit or coarse builder's sand to improve drainage. Layer on three or four inches of aged manure and compost, then add another inch of sand for the bulbs to sit on. Their roots can easily reach the nutritional layer of soil, yet excess water will drain away quickly.

Another important element in lily care is letting them ripen properly after blooming. Both stems and foliage should ripen to a rich brown before they are cleared away. This triggers the storage of nutrients in the bulb, ensuring an adequate food supply for winter root growth. Seedpods should be removed when tiny so that seed production won't sap energy from the bulbs. It's fine to trim off the browning stems a few inches at a time, but don't rush things by cutting off anything green.

Happy lilies of all kinds can get far taller than expected, so it's wise to provide some support. My favorite stakes are made of rebar, which quickly rusts to an unobtrusive cinnamon color and can stay in place all year round. To support a group of three to five lilies, bend ten feet of quarter-inch rebar into a half-hoop (a 55-gallon drum makes a great shaping mold), using a pipe wrench to make a smooth curve.

Aromatic Annuals

Some of the sweetest scents in the summer garden come from inexpensive annuals. Mignonette and Sweet William (which can also be biennial or perennial), sweet peas and sweet alyssum all have pleasing odors in their own right, but they also combine deliciously to create drifts of more intricate perfumes that tantalize the nose by day or night. For the most part, annuals are easy to grow. Give them decent soil, adequate water, and a minimum of half a day of sun, and they will perform unstintingly all summer long. The hardest-blooming sorts—like violas and petunias—will remain active longer if given a timed-release fertilizer like Osmocote. Alternatively, you can feed them with a water-soluble fertilizer every week to extend their peak performance.

Be aware, however, that aroma in annuals has sometimes been lost as hybridizers focus on creating larger flowers or a longer bloom period. Sweet peas are a classic case in point; once a byword for fragrance, they are now as apt to be scentless as to be redolent of romance.

Stocks, too, are still famous for their spicy clove perfume, yet in some strains, it is so mild as to be unnoticeable a few feet away. Likewise, modern snapdragons may have a pungent, velvety odor or no scent at all. (To my nose, the dark, midnight red ones smell the best, with a rich, almost peppery sweetness, like chili jam.) To assure yourself of a satisfyingly sweet summer, perform the sniff test at the nursery and bring home only strongly scented plants.

Give annuals

a quick start by

using rich but

well-drained potting

soil lightened with

vermiculite and

coarse sand.

When a recent move shrank my garden from acres to what felt like mere inches, my immediate response was to fill a few large containers with fragrant annuals. As gardeners who are spatially challenged already know, one can cram quite a large garden into a very small space this way. No matter how bitty the yard, there is always room for another pot or two, even if it means walking down paths or steps crab-wise so as not to disturb the packed and spreading pots. Actually, when the crowded containers are jammed with aromatic herbs and fragrant flowers, it encourages healthy interspecies contact, because brushing against them releases such a happy rush of scents.

However limited one's space may be, a few fragrance favorites will always make the cut. Foremost amongst these for me is mignonette (*Reseda odora*, to 1'), a French nickname meaning 'little darling'. Undeniably frumpy, its frizzy green and brown flowers smell like the breath of heaven. Light but penetrating, carrying but not cloying, the fragrance pervades the garden on warm, still days and lingers long into the night. Like so many of us, this plant is nothing much to look at, yet remarkable in essence.

Finding your own favorites, both singly and in combination, is part of the fascination of growing fra-

grant plants of all kinds. Annuals are especially fun, providing instant gratification at such a reasonable price that we can afford to splash them all over the garden without suffering pangs of acquisitor's guilt. So many deliciously fragrant annuals are available that endless lists become ridiculous. The best way to discover them is by making frequent trips to nurseries, where you can indulge your taste for floral sweetness without harm—indeed, even in excess, it seems rather to promote health and happiness. I offer you, therefore, a happy handful of fragrant annuals that my own summer garden is never without. Remember, too, that a great many excitingly scented annuals (and other plants) are night-fragrant, so a browse through Chapter Six may also expand your ideas about concocting summery perfumes.

Sweet Alyssum

Humble as a daisy, annual sweet alyssum (*Lobularia maritima*, to 1') is one of those plants you only buy once, for it seeds itself about with artless abandon. Fortunately, the seedlings are very easy to uproot, should they land where you don't want them. However, sweet alyssum has a happy knack for placement, tucking itself into the corner of the steps or beneath a sheltering perennial, where its netted stems and tiny foliage are no detriment. Sweet alyssum begins to bloom in early spring, carrying on until winter frosts turn the tiny white flowers black overnight. Where they are protected, the little tussocks just keep on blooming straight through the year, renewing themselves without assistance from the gardener. Pretty but not showy, sweet alyssum makes a foamy edger along beds and pathways, pouring out its heavy scent of warm honey, and pleasing bees and humans alike. The variously colored forms are far less fragrant than the species, which is as good a mixer in floral perfumes as in garden beds.

CALIFORNIA MARIGOLD

Tall and bushy as a border shrub, California marigold (*Tagetes lemmonii*, 3–6') is also unassuming to look at, yet offers an exceptional scent to passing hands. Its finely dissected leaves make a lacy thicket, studded at the stem tips with tiny, tangerine-colored single marigolds. Both flowers and foliage are permeated with a remarkable herbal perfume that mingles mellow spearmint and spicy marigold with tangy lemon and a hint of orange.

In the cooler parts of the Pacific Northwest, this tender perennial is grown as an annual, but it often winters over in dry, sunny sites, where it may also seed itself about in a modest way. Lean soils and plenty of sun make for compact plants with a scent so strong that some people find it objectionable. I like to plant it at the edge of the border or along paths I take daily, where I can brush against the fragrant filigree till it scents my clothing. One year, I paired it with South African honey bush (*Melianthus major*), a boldly scaled perennial with silver-blue, sawtoothed leaves that smell like peanut butter when touched. That combination, I have to say, was more memorable than felicitous. However, when this robust marigold was partnered with purple sage, *Salvia officinalis* 'Purpurascens', and bronze fennel, *Foeniculum vulgare* 'Bronze Form', the olfactory result was as happy as the visual effect.

My all-time favorite marigold is a true annual called 'Lulu' (to 1'). This cheerful creature has wiry, netted foliage tipped with little yellow pompoms. I love to ruffle this plant, for both flowers and foliage have an invigorating fragrance. Clean, bright, and uplifting, Lulu smells like good humor—not the ice cream sort, but the kind that comes with a peaceful mind and a merry heart. A single well-fed plant will fill a twelve-inch pot to bursting in a few weeks, blooming its heart out all summer

*South African honey bush (*Melianthus major*) needs a warm, dry spot in well-drained soil.*

long. Generosity is as appealing in plants as it is in people, and little Lulu has proved lastingly attractive over the years.

SWEET PEAS

Beautifully crisp and ruffled annual sweet peas (*Lathyrus odoratus*) can be disappointing despite providing masses of flowers, for some of the prettiest kinds lack much scent. That's because English sweet pea fanciers are serious fanatics, dedicated largely to form. They have indeed elevated the humble cottage garden sweet pea to truly giddy heights, but along the way, that familiar, evocative scent has been diminished or lost altogether. (Much the same thing happened to roses during their mid-twentieth-century hybridizing boom.)

Fortunately, fragrance fans have also been hard at work, selecting and sedulously maintaining potently perfumed sweet peas. As a result, several excellent old-fashioned seed strains are now available. The loveliest for cutting is an English one called 'Antique Fantasy', which blooms in fascinating watercolor tints, from deep blues and purples to wines and clear reds, as well as pinks and creams, lavender and lilac. Smaller and less ruffled, the flowers are less refined than show-quality named forms, but they have all the potency of perfume that show blossoms often lack. There are, of course, a few named forms with astonishing scents, including 'White Supreme' (fabulously expensive but fabulous), milky blue 'Maggie May', and lilac 'Marion'.

Other deliciously scented sweet pea strains include 'Cupid', a low-growing carpeter to replace the much-touted 'Snoopea', a sprawler that offers big flowers in bright, clean colors but very little fragrance.

Drape the inside of a picket (or any) fence with black plastic bird netting, securing it with wood staples. Now your sweet peas will quickly scale the heights, supported firmly but unobtrusively. ❧

'Cupid' blossoms are also clear and splashy, and their scent is splendid. So, too, is 'Jet Set Mixed', which provides big, zippy, hot-toned flowers with plenty of perfume. The Thompson & Morgan seed catalog (see Appendix Two, "Resources") offers its own 'T & M Prize Strain Mixed' of very ruffled, large-flowered Spencer types chosen as much for their fragrance as for form and habit. (The Spencers are an aristocratic bunch, first bred by Lady Di's great-grandfather's head gardener—but as a strain, they too have been developed more for looks than for fragrance.)

Scented Carpets

Quite a few fragrant plants are carpeters, plants that spread in relatively flat sheets over bed or pathway. The sturdiest of them can take a fair amount of foot traffic, but in areas where many feet pass on a regular basis, it's wise to add stepping stones for relief. Where little walking will occur, a small field of mint makes a sumptuous carpet, and few plants cover ground more willingly. What's more, there are literally dozens of fragrant and flavorful forms to choose amongst, from classic peppermint or spearmint to lemon or orange, cinnamon or apple, or even pineapple.

Silvery variegated apple mint (*Mentha rotundifolia* 'Variegata', to 18") is mannerly and good-looking, spreading decorously into sheets of Irish green, each leaf iced with a frosty white edge, each stem tipped with pink and white flower heads. This is one of the few mints that can be kept under control in the garden proper. Most others are best used as carpeters or confined to pots, which are in turn set into solid saucers to prevent their questing roots from escaping through the drainage holes.

Where a truly flat carpet is wanted, creeping Corsican mint, *M. requienii*, pours between pavers in mossy sheets less than an inch high. Too delicate to withstand much trampling on its own, it is a terrific filler for

Above Left *Late bloom-ing, long-stemmed* Primula florindae *has ornamental seed-pods as well as spice-cookie scented blossoms in soft shades of yellow, cin-namon, and tawny orange.* **Above Right** *Since silky poppies have no scent of their own, pair them with perfumed partners like this haze of creamy sea kale,* Crambe cordifolia, *which smells like honey and ripe pears.* **Left** *Chinese beauty bush,* Kolkwitzia amabilis, *makes a stunning backdrop in late spring, when its creamy pink trumpets spill their triumphant sweet-ness on the warming air.*

Above Left *Pure white 'Casa Blanca' lilies fill the late garden with their intense, saturated perfume.*
Above Right *Cherry pie,* Heliotropium arborescens, *a richly scented tender perennial, opens its velvety blue flowers all winter when given a warm, sunny windowsill.* **Right** *Lemon catmint,* Nepeta citriodora, *lends an aromatic briskness to the heady sweetness of clove pinks (*Dianthus). **Below** *A hazy scrim of hair grass,* Deschampsia flexuosa, *frames the marshmallow scented blossoms of* Malva moschata *'Grandiflora', which bloom all summer long.*

Above Left *Beautiful but rowdy and utterly undisciplined, Queen Anne's lace (*Daucus carota*) should be yanked from the border the minute it stops smelling like cream soda to prevent indiscriminate seeding.* **Above Right** *Satiny and sleek, the apricot and ginger coloring of* Rosa *'Just Joey' is echoed in its tangy perfume, which has bright, citrusy overtones.* **Right** *Deadly poisonous and astonishingly beautiful,* Datura *(currently* Brugmansia*) 'Charles Grimaldi' has a literally intoxicating fragrance that makes every day a party.*

Above Left *Elegantly drooping Abyssinian gladiolus (presently known as* Gladiolus callianthus) *bloom late and long, scenting the autumn garden with incense and golden syrup.* **Above Right** *This delicious garden melange is scented by the silvery stars of the non-climbing* Clematis recta, *which bloom from late spring to midsummer.* **Right** *A whole host of flowers are mildly fragrant, offering their sweetness only to those who examaine them closely, such as this astilbe hybrid.*

crazy paving or stepping stones, where its rather culinary scent—a blend of mint and cooking sage—is released by passing feet. It also adds a happy sparkle of scent to carpets of creeping thymes (except in very hot sites, where it may scorch).

Thymes come in as wide a range of scents and flavors as mints and are far less invasive. Specialty nurseries can provide carpeting or clumping thymes that smell and taste of lemon or orange blossom, of caraway seed or lavender, among many other things. Creeping thymes may be variegated with silver or gold, softly chartreuse or vividly yellow, grey or olive or sage, or a lustrous bottle green. In flower, a seed-sown carpet of creeping mother of thyme (*Thymus serpyllum*) becomes a heathery, tweedy tapestry flecked with rose and pink, lavender and cream. Herb nurseries can offer several dozen forms that will give you a full palette of flower colors to play with, from the chalky pink of 'Annie Hall' to the rose red of 'Coccineus', plum purple 'Mountain', or salmony 'Pink Chintz'.

Sprinkle a mixture of creeping thyme seeds over an open, sunny site to get a bumpy carpet of heathery greens and greys, studded with tiny flowers. ꙮ

All smell cheerfully herbal when brushed or trod upon, but to increase both textural and olfactory interest, add a few clumps of scintillating lemon thyme, *T.* × *citriodorus*, to the living rug. Outstanding in the garden for year-round good looks and pleasant scent, lemon thyme has endless kitchen uses as well. My favorite amongst a multitude of attractive forms is silver lemon thyme, 'Argenteus Variegatus'. A compact subshrub (to 10"), it has slender leaves primly edged with white, and fizzy little flowers of pale lilac. Another pet is 'Fragrantissima', a dapper shrubette (to 10") with pink and cream flowers and velvety grey leaves that smell of oranges.

Woolly thyme, *T. lanuginosus*, feels delightfully soft underfoot, and you can choose either the sage-grey,

pink-flowered species or the greyer, lavender-flowered 'Halls' Variety'. Woolly thyme smells especially aromatic when interplanted with Corsican mint (*Mentha requienii*) and pungent, prostrate beach wormwood, *Artemisia stelleriana* 'Silver Brocade'.

SCENTED CARPETING STRAWBERRY

A few years ago, England's Blooms of Bressingham nursery introduced an evergreen, ornamental strawberry that smells nicer than most strawberries taste. A cross between a kitchen garden strawberry and a perennial cinquefoil (*Potentilla 'Miss Willmott'*), *Fragaria frel* 'Pink Panda' produces masses of exceptionally fragrant pink flowers the size of a quarter from May through November. Don't be disappointed if you find very few fruits on these ardent spreaders, for the berries tend to be mealy and rather tasteless. Enjoy 'Pink Panda' for its scent and color, and put it where it can spill luxuriantly over the edge of a wall or race along a walkway. A few plants will send out crowds of little runners that will replace themselves in turn, weaving a lacy web of plants in very short order.

Like all strawberries, 'Pink Panda' appreciates full sun, but it will bloom generously in partial shade, especially where the soil is deep and not too dry. It also makes a splendid pot plant, tumbling in long, scented streamers beneath rosy trumpet lilies, aromatic, grey-green lavender, and plump spikes of pink or lilac hyssop.

CARPETING CHAMOMILE

Perhaps the most traditional herbal carpeter is chamomile—not the annual kind called German, but the finer-textured perennial sold as Roman chamomile (*Anthemis nobilis*). Used as a fragrant lawn substitute for centuries, Roman chamomile stays vividly green in hot summers when grasses fade to brown, needing little or no supplementary water except during extended droughts.

Once established, chamomile remains thick and trim with only an occasional mowing (which smells gorgeous), and holds up well under moderate foot traffic. It grows most luxuriantly in well-drained soils and full sun, but may look a bit scruffy in shady areas. In heavy soils, it tends to rot out in patches over the winter, so you may want to mix it with other plants, perhaps grass daisies, *Bellis perennis*, some clover, and several kinds of creeping thyme.

   If you want to make tea from your chamomile, look for seed or plants of *Matricaria recutita* instead. Sweet and mild on its own, annual chamomile is highly compatible in the teapot, blending sympathetically with dozens of more potently flavorful herbs. Among my own favorite chamomile companions is lemon balm (*Melissa officinalis*), a plain-faced herb with a lilting, zesty fragrance that lifts sagging spirits. Just as a slice of lemon makes chamomile tea magic rather than just mild, mingled scents of chamomile and lemon balm in the garden are similarly synergistic. An inveterate self-sower, lemon balm is handsomest and most restrained in its golden form, 'All Gold'. This one has bright yellow leaves in spring that soften to old gold by midsummer. It self-seeds moderately, and its children will be a mix of gilded and plain green.

Add a few sprigs of lemon balm to a bottle of white wine vinegar, and set it in a warm place for a few weeks to mellow. ∿

Upright Aromatic Herbs

When high summer fills the garden with astonishing perfumes, the effect, though highly romantic, can be a bit much. The blended scents of roses and lilies, mignonette and heliotrope become more complex and less overwhelming when tempered with brisker aromatics such as artemisia and rosemary. Spicy

bee balm, soothing chamomile, and mellow lavender add depth and softness to treacle-sweet jasmine and trumpet lilies. Sugary roses smell richer for the contrast of pungent sage and the natural lemon-pepper of California marigold (*Tagetes lemmonii*), while colorful forms of basil are just as good at mixing in the border as they are in summery salads.

Indeed, herbs offer us a wide range of olfactory experiences, indoors and out. Toss in a handful of fragrant herb leaves, and plain bath water becomes tranquilizing (chamomile), stimulating (rosemary and lavender), or outright sensual (rose geranium, spearmint, and lemon balm). This last combination creates an especially enticing garden perfume, and works as nicely in the teapot as in the tub.

In the garden, hardworking herbs can decorate less-than-ideal places. Naturally, new plants need regular watering, but once established and showing new growth, woody herbs will thrive in dry places, happily taking all the sun they can get. Poor, lean soils suit many herbs right down to the ground, while reflected heat from neighboring apartments or from the street leave them lush rather than limp. Mediterranean natives such as sage and rosemary, lavender and thyme love the hot spots along the driveway or by the pool. Many fragrant cooking herbs like basil, coriander (cilantro), and lemon balm will also cope in warm places, but perform better with supplemental water when summer temperatures climb.

Lemon Verbena

Semievergreen, slim-leaved lemon verbena, *Aloysia triphylla*, may be a tender pot plant or a good garden shrub, depending on where you live. In cold-winter areas, this aromatic foliage plant is best housed in a generous pot so that it can spend the chilly months in a comfortable kitchen or sheltered sun porch. Elsewhere, lemon verbena is perfectly hardy (indeed, it can be coddled along in Seattle gardens, if given a cozy corner and excellent drainage). Leggy by nature, lemon verbenas can be trained into lovely little lollipop-headed standards (multitrunked ones are especially fun, looking like Dr. Seuss creatures). You can also pinch them back in youth to encourage bushiness, but you will still end up with a fairly airy shrub.

Beloved ingredients in potpourri, herb teas, sorbets, and jellies, skinny lemon verbena leaves are also invaluable elements in garden perfumes. Brush them with your hand to release the captivating scent of lemons with a touch of honey, as refreshing on a hot summer day as in depths of winter. Pink-flowered lemon catmint, *Calamintha citriodora*, makes a pleasing companion for lemon verbena. This bushy perennial has a complex, mint-and-citrus fragrance that clings to our cats' fur (they love to sleep beneath it). The leaves bring a similar flavor and a relaxing, slightly soporific effect to the teapot.

Lemon verbena is invaluable in garden perfumes: brush it with your hand to release the captivating scent. ᑲ

PINEAPPLE AND FRUIT SAGES

The red flowers of upright, bushy pineapple sage, *Salvia elegans* (to 3'), are as attractive to humming-birds as the fuzzy grey leaves are to humans. Large and velvety, the leaves are invitingly strokable, rewarding the touch with wafts of delectably fruity fragrance. The somewhat more tender fruit sage, *Salvia dorisiana* (to 4'), is similarly felty and fragrant of leaf, with an even more interesting scent that suggests fruit salad. In both cases, the long leaves taste as good as they smell, and can be added to fruit salads, iced or hot herb teas, and sorbets. The flowers of fruit sage are also highly attractive to hummingbirds, who bicker loudly about territorial rights when this silvery plant is in bloom.

Shrubby Cleveland sage, *Salvia clevelandii* (2–4'), is a California native with splendidly aromatic foliage. In the garden, it makes a mounded, grey-green shrub, threaded with spikes of soft blue flowers, which smell as good as the supple leaves. Where colder temperatures prevail, it does nicely in a pot, wintering over happily in a sunny window. Indoors, it will scent a whole room with its curious aroma, which recalls very good cherry tobacco.

English or culinary sage, *Salvia officinalis* (to 2'), is an excellent mixer in every way. Its smooth fragrance complements anything you put it with, just as its dapper, grey-green foliage and rounded form enhance any perennial in the garden. Grey and sleek 'Berggarten' is the most handsome form, producing spikes of fragrant, dark blue flowers in early summer. Splendidly colored 'Purpurascens' has matte purple leaves and purple flowers set in dark red bracts, a delightful companion for sweetly scented ornamental onions like 'Purple Sensation' or for 'Mabel Violet' lilies. 'Tricolor' sage is streaked with cream and pink and soft green, while 'Icterina' is a cheerful lemon and lime blend. All remain under two feet tall but may spread as much as four feet across in time.

ROSEMARY, LAVENDER, AND OREGANO

Rosemary (*Rosmarinus officinalis*) comes in a goodly range of sizes and shapes, with flowers that may be blue or lavender, pink or white. Flowing 'Prostratus' makes a spicily fragrant groundcover that spills over the lip of a wall like living water, while staunchly upright 'Tuscan Blue' will stand sentinel by doorway or garden gate. Compact and shapely, 'Benenden Blue' has ocean-colored blossoms, as does trim little 'Huntingdon Blue', a mannerly form suitable for the smallest or most formal of gardens. Large and lustrous rosemaries look remarkably beautiful when threaded with scented clematis, which can scramble over and through the sturdy shrubs. Smaller

rosemaries partner well with tall trumpet lilies, shading their moisture-loving roots while letting their heads reach the sun. Rosemary smells and looks especially beautiful when grouped with fine-textured columns of fennel and billows of lavender.

Lavenders, too, come in all shapes and sizes. Among the smallest are dwarf *Lavandula angustifolia* 'Hidcote' (to 1'), a grey-leaved form with dark purple flowers, and 'Munstead' (to 14"), with green foliage and periwinkle blue flowers. Taller 'Jean Davis' (to 2') has chalky pink flowers, while plump little 'Twickle Purple' makes a pillow of purple in midsummer. Hardy and handsome, 'Fred Boutin' (to 3') offers sea-blue flowers on very long stems that are much prized for making lavender bunches and braids. Lavenders get blowsy and overblown in just a few years, so it's a good idea to keep young replacements growing on in the nursery bed. Older plants can be clipped to encourage bushiness, but use a light hand, for cutting back to old wood results in permanent bare patches.

Ornamental oreganos make fat cushions of color in bed or border, and add their warm, strong fragrance to summery garden perfumes. Some look like escapees from the kitchen garden, but dusky, maroon-leaved *Origanum laevigatum* 'Herrenhausen' (18") looks decidedly exotic, spinning out in great wheels of subfusc foliage tipped with mahogany flowers. Border oreganos like sunny *Origanum vulgare* 'Aureum' (to 2') and cream-splashed 'Variegatum' spill in cascading mounds, their airy purple florets clustered at the tips of arching stems. Ornamental hybrids like 'Hopley's Purple' and 'Kent Beauty' are modest-looking creepers that send up sheaves of small flowers set in

Cut long wands

of 'Fred Boutin'

lavender, bind them

softly, then bend the

stems back over

the flowers and bind

again, creating a

green 'cage' of

blossoms. ❧

showy bracts tinted lavender, rose, mauve, or purple. These dry nicely, retaining color and scent well both in the garden and when picked for craft use.

These and other adaptable herbs thrive in dry, torrid summers yet take cool or rainy ones in stride. Many herbs show a tendency to sprawl in wet summers, but a good clipping will prompt bushy second growth that remains tidy through autumn. Mounders like oregano and basil, mint and marjoram, savory and tarragon, dill and sage, should all be sheared back in August. Woody herbs, too, such as rosemary and lavender, sage and horehound, can be cut back a bit to tighten their texture and promote fresh growth. These, however, must be trimmed with a lighter hand, for if taken back to old (bare) wood, they rarely if ever recover.

Chapter
Four

4

AUTUMN
FRAGRANCES

September, October,
November

For gardeners, fall is less an ending than the beginning of another great cycle of work and rest and fulfillment. In fall, we plant the bulbs that will illuminate the spring yet unborn. In fall, we dig and divide and recombine our plants into fresh combinations to enjoy next summer. In fall, we commit new plants to the ground, giving trees, shrubs, and perennials a chance to make strong root growth before winter. In fall, we can relax and let our plants ripen into maturity before they sleep.

Autumn is also glorious in its own right. As the night air cools, leaves catch fire, the tired greens igniting to lava reds, ember oranges, and smoldering copper. As the slanting daylight lengthens, it gilds the garden with a soft haze. Numinous and transcendent, the autumn light turns mess into magic. When we can appreciate that the slumping, seed-spangled demise of summer's magnificence is truly magnificent in itself, it becomes easier to stop being so concerned about grooming away every browning leaf. Instead, we can relax and simply revel in autumn's richness.

A delightfully large part of this sensory richness is olfactory, for the smells of fall rank among its greatest splendors. Ripening plums and pears and apples release lovely, fruity odors. The kitchen garden offers musky tomatoes, piquant fennel, pungent basil. After a warm summer (not always a given in maritime areas), the aging leaves of certain strawberries and sweet violets smell as delicious as their own fruits and flowers. The tumbling hearts of browning katsura leaves (*Cercidiphyllum japonicum*) have a milky, caramel scent, one rather weirdly echoed in the mahogany red fruits of pagoda bush (*Leycesteria formosa*), which taste exactly like slightly scorched homemade butterscotch.

Autumn brings dozens of floral smells to appreciate. Late phlox sends its spicy, warm-cookie scent wafting through the garden. Honey-edged buddleia mint adds

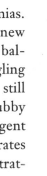

sparkle and zest to the velvety, dark perfume of petunias. Bitter-sweet chrysanthemums (whatever their new names, I will always think of them by the old one) balance the heady bouquet of late roses and lilies mingling with the blue-belled clematis 'Mrs. Robert Bryden', still going strong after several months in bloom. Shrubby *Clerodendrum trichotomum* pours out its thick, effulgent perfume, while the tatty Queen Anne's lace that decorates roadside verges and shaggy meadows still smells penetratingly of cream soda.

Below you'll find a list of a few of the more reliable late-season fragrance plants. To discover others, cruise nurseries and the gardens of friends, paying attention with your nose as well as with your eyes to what's there. Plenty of late bloomers are to be had when we begin to seek them out in earnest. If few are strongly fragrant, several offer pleasant smells that blend happily with summer leftovers—fragrant annuals like sweet alyssum, nicotiana, and mignonette, perennial phlox and chocolate cosmos, several late lilies, lots of roses. Indeed, once we stop fixating on having the garden ready for bed unseasonably early, we find a treasure trove of persistent bloomers that carry on until frost.

Abyssinian Gladiolas

Elegant, lovely, and long-blooming, the Abyssinian gladiolus is one of those inexpensive bulbs that can be planted at intervals (in pots or in the ground) to bloom over a very long period. Long sold as *Acidanthera murielae* (2–3'), this richly fragrant South African is now officially called *Gladiolus bicolor* 'Murielae', so its bulbs may be labeled with either of these names. Tall and showy, these striking plants present arching, pleated foliage in wide ribbons all summer, topped in August and September by flowers like outsized garden gladiolas. The white flowers curve on long, graceful

necks, their petals splashed deep into their throats with wine-red stains. They give off a joyfully seductive perfume, which deepens to new warmth by night. It is fascinating to watch the florets open on a sunny day, unfolding in little pulsing rushes, much like Oriental poppies.

Happily adaptable in mild-winter areas, these rather tender bulbs elsewhere demand good soil with excellent drainage and plenty of sun. Even then, they tend to vanish over the winter in heavy soils. Since they are so cheap, those of us blessed with clay-based gardens can just regard them as obliging annuals. (Bulbs planted as late as June will bloom in late summer or early autumn.)

Sheaves of elegant,

creamy Abyssinian

gladiolas make

sumptuous company

for late-flowering

windflowers.

Occasionally, when well pleased, they will multiply instead of dwindle, even seeding in for lucky gardeners. In my Seattle garden, they loved the southwest-facing hillside. Threaded between sprawling Mediterranean herbs such as rosemary, sage, and lavender, these dapper bulbs actually colonized, despite the acid clay they grew in. It's always worth playing about with plants you really like, experimenting with placement until you find a spot they enjoy. For this reason (certainly not for mere greed), it's an excellent idea to buy plants in multiples rather than onesies. Write the cost off to scientific research—but do keep track of your results in a

garden journal, so you can both remember your information (it's amazing how much unforgettable stuff we do forget) and share it with others.

Butterfly Bush

*I*f regularly deadheaded (once a month is fine), summer-blooming butterfly bushes (*Buddleia* spp.) will bloom well into fall, when the profusely fragrant flowers become even more so. Coarse of leaf and leggy of line, buddleias are seldom outstandingly handsome shrubs. They look best when chopped hard to the ground each year (a chore for late winter or earliest spring). If you want more height from your buddleias, you can stump them back to a permanent framework of trunk and main branches some two or three feet high. This way, the plants will be bushier and the flowers more profuse. These, after all, are the main event here. Smelling of honey and hay, the long, spiky flower heads bloom like summery lilacs in shades of lavender and blue, rose and pink, cream or white. They really are irresistible to butterflies; in my garden, the swallowtails will cluster so thickly on a heavily blooming buddleia that you can scarcely see the blossoms.

Harlequin Glory Bower

*I*t's very clear why shrubby *Clerodendrum trichoto-mum* is called glory bower, for its gracefully curving branches do indeed form a bower of leaf and exceptionally fragrant flower. (The "harlequin" part is harder to understand, for that name is usually given to variegated plants, which this is not.) A multitrunked, deciduous shrub or small tree ten to fifteen feet tall, glory bower has long, tapered oval leaves trimmed with tufts of tubular, creamy blossoms that exude a truly astonishing perfume. When given light shade and rich soil, glory

bower grows quite quickly, its arching arms making a natural cave, which can be underplanted with evergreen ferns and hellebores and masses of spring bulbs. The flowers are followed by fat little fruits of a glossy, metallic blue set amid rosy calyxes left behind when the flowers fall. Its scent is so strong that it overpowers most would-be companion fragrances at once. (However, at a nursery on Vashon Island, near Seattle, this shrub is grown at the edge of a terrace filled with enormous potted daturas; see Chapter Six, "Night-Fragrant Plants"). As the afternoon draws on, the daturas begin to spill their own remarkable and penetrating scent, and the combination of the two is truly memorable.

Chrysanthemums

Chrysanthemums are indispensable in autumn color schemes, where their bronzed tints bolster the storm-cloud blues and purples of asters and coppery goldenrods. ❧

In recent years, busy botanists have frolicked amongst these late bloomers, happily dividing what you and I were content to call mums into *Chrysanthemum*, *Dendranthemum*, *Leucanthemum*, *Matricaria*, and a few other species. This has happened before—lumpers and splitters are always at war—but last time the lumpers won. Now, taxonomic revisions have again destroyed the pleasant simplicity of this big clan, so now we have to hunt down old favorites in various new (or sometimes really old) locations. For instance, that old garden standby *Chrysanthemum coreanum* is now *Dendranthemum* × *grandiflorum*, while Shasta daisies, long *C. maximum*, are once again *Leucanthemum* × *superbum*. Fortunately, like roses, they smell just as good whatever their names.

Among the best of the fragrant late bloomers in the chrysanthemum family

are hybrids, which conveniently continue to be known by a single name. One such is 'Innocence', a tall (to 2') charmer in pink and ivory, which looks very lovely in front of a cluster of late-flowering rubrum lilies and the rosy leaves of a pink-stemmed cutleaf maple, *Acer japonicum* 'Orido Nishiki'. Tawny pink 'Bronze Elegance' (18") and dainty, button-flowered 'Mei Kyo' (14") swirl in pungent waves beneath long-flowering roses like toasty cinnamon-sugar 'Charles Austin' or ginger-whip 'Just Joey'. The sharp, clean scent of chrysanthemums cuts the heaviness of roses and lilies, but also combines excitingly with the scent of zippy herbs like curry plant, *Helichrysum angustifolium*, a silvery sprawler with highly aromatic foliage, as well as mints and various artemisias.

Chocolate Sunflower

Tall and graceful, the willowleaf sunflower (*Helianthus salicifolius*, 6–10') makes an upright sheaf of soft gold in late summer and autumn. Its skinny-petaled yellow flowers smell enticingly of dark chocolate, with a deeper scent than the Swiss Miss milkiness of chocolate cosmos (see Chapter Three, "Summer Fragrances"). This sturdy prairie plant likes plenty of sun and ordinary soils and thrives with little or no supplementary water once established. It dislikes crowding neighbors, but can be underplanted with airy bugbanes (the *Cimicifuga* clan, themselves deliciously scented) and pungent chrysanthemums.

Sweet Bugbanes

The common name "bugbane" gives us no hint of the multiple attractions of the handsome *Cimicifuga* family. The most strongly scented are derived from a native American species, *C. racemosa*, which raises its sinuous white wands packed with small,

warmly scented flowers above lacy foliage from late summer into autumn. This plant has several named forms, loveliest of which is the dark-leaved 'Purpurea'. A similar-looking cousin, the European *C. ramosa*, has pale pink flowers with only mild fragrance. A notable exception is the fabled 'Brunette', a black-leaved beauty with a strong and carrying scent rather like clover and honey. Although its long, slim bottlebrush flowers are pale pink, it likely owes its striking fragrance to a touch of American blood somewhere back in its ancestry. Most years, bugbanes don't really hit their stride until mid-September, when their delicate scent becomes pronounced and almost heavy. They make attractive underskirts for late roses, and their spilling sweetness makes them good candidates for container plantings by patio or terrace. Plant one next to an upright, nonclimbing *Clematis stans* to create a dazzling floral fragrance.

Clematis

A recent import from China, *Clematis stans* has a bold leaf rather like the earlier-blooming, upright *C. heracleifolia* or the similar *C. h.* var. *davidiana*. Because it doesn't climb, its lanky arms need to be tied to slim stakes (bamboo wands do nicely) that can support its three- to four-foot length. From late summer well into autumn, those long arms are spangled with little bursts of soft, porcelain blue flowers that exude a warm, delicately floral perfume with hints of honey, lemon, and vanilla. It does nicely in bed or border, but is especially useful in pots or containers, which can be moved near seating areas as the fragrance develops. Best of all, it blooms well in light or filtered shade, making it a great choice where direct sunlight is limited. (It also accepts full sun with equanimity.)

Quite a few of the showy summer-blooming clematis will rebloom nicely come fall, notably sky blue

'Will Goodwin' and the creamy-eyed, Wedgwood blue 'Lady Betty Balfour'. When the tightly doubled, royal purple 'Vyvyan Pennell' reblooms in September, its second crop of flowers are often only loosely double or even single, and may be rather lighter in color as well. Not intensely fragrant, they offer up a light, softly floral scent that rounds out the low-toned, resonant scents of sage and lavender. The pale blue bells of 'Mrs. Robert Bryden' are still profuse and deliciously scented in September, making a wonderful counterpoint to the deep fragrance of silvery mauve 'Angel Face' roses. Several species of clematis are ardent fall bloomers, notably primula-scented *Clematis rehderiana*, with its splayed, greeny yellow bell flowers, lemony *C. serratifolia*, and banana yellow *C. tangutica*. Any of these last can be draped through a hedge (preferably a loose, unclipped one) or allowed to lace through low-growing perennials. Grown this way, their delicate flowers and light fragrance can be appreciated close at hand. Threaded with late-blooming bulbs like Abyssinian gladiolus or crinum lilies, these scented clematis weave themselves into textured tapestries that linger well into winter, when their silky seed heads are as decorative as the flowers.

Clematis 'Mrs. Robert Bryden' blooms long and late, but requires significant support to do so gracefully. ❧

Milk-and-Wine Lily

First cousin to the amaryllis, the milk-and-wine lily, *Crinum bulbispermum*, has a similar arrangement of strappy leaves and tall (to 20") bloom spikes, each tipped with clusters of trumpet-shaped blossoms. Its milky white petals are striped with wine red in the usual form, but named selections like 'Pam's Pink' and 'Roseum' are solidly colored. In Northwestern gardens, crinums bloom from late summer

into fall, when their liltingly fragrant flowers are most welcome.

Like most South African bulbs, these do best in rich but well-drained soils, and although they will flower when grown in light shade, they are far more productive when given what passes for full sun here in the Northwest, especially in maritime regions. When well suited, crinums are reliably hardy and attractively ever-green, but in shady or cooler gardens, they are best grown in pots and given winter shelter in a dry garage or an unheated sun porch. I must say that they detest my crowded garden, returning with reluctance and sulking a good deal after a wet winter. Other gardeners, however, succeed brilliantly with these lovely lilies, so do have a shot at pleasing them, for they make a decidedly worthy addition to the fragrant garden.

Hardy Cyclamen

*H*ardy Neapolitan cyclamen (*Cyclamen neapoli-tanum*) begins to flower in late summer, but really comes into its own in September, when the rounded corms are buried under swarms of reflexed, fuchsia-pink flowers. Their wild, sweet fragrance is strongest on warm, still afternoons, but is always perceptible if you bend down and examine the flowers closely. It is well worth the trouble to prostrate yourself before these enchanting creatures, for the detail-ing of their construction is extraordinary. At close hand, you can observe the way the color deepens about the fluted tucks of petal that surround their narrow throats, changing from mauve and lavender to bur-gundy and rose. The fascinatingly marbled leaves appear with the first flowers, but not until October

Since wild cyclamen are becoming endangered, buy them only from nurseries that grow them from seed. ❧

do they arrive *en masse* to replace the flowers with a splendidly patterned tapestry.

Hardy cyclamen thrive in deep, well-drained soils enriched with plenty of humus. They do very well in dry, often shady spots, and are one of the few plants that genuinely enjoy life when planted at the base of mature trees. Plant cyclamen shallowly, never more than an inch or two deep, topping them off with aged manure or compost. Don't worry, however, if the fat corms push themselves above the soil surface after a few years; they know what they are doing. Continue to supply a shallow annual feeding mulch, but let them find their own level.

Wild Strawberry

A scented carpet of European wild strawberries makes another autumnal treat, spilling in fragrant green lacework from pots or foaming around autumn crocus or crinums. Unlike their dainty cousins the tiny alpine strawberries, wild strawberries (*Fragaria vesca*) are plump and perfumed. Rather than the typical red, these fruits have a yellow skin blushed with rose. When ripe, wild strawberries produce a powerfully sweet scent that is detectable at a considerable distance. Their flavor, however, is somewhat odd, with deep, mysterious undertones that are generally described as musklike. Never having tasted musk, I can't verify that, but wild strawberries do have a savory component that sweet strawberries lack. When baked by hot autumn sun, and again after a nipping frost, the drying leaves give off the characteristic jammy scent of ripe strawberries blended with a darker, woodsy scent which some again liken to musk and others to Russian leather. To my nose, it is the scent of fall itself, that of death and slow decay—not the nasty stink of rotting things, but the clean smell of forest duff.

Witch Hazel

As a child, I loved to roam the woods near my home, looking for flowers and watching the seasons pass. While my favorite season has always been whichever one is current, growing up in New England gave me a special delight in autumn, when the trees clothe themselves with transcendent beauty. (Indeed, I lived in Concord, Massachusetts, where the Transcendentalist movement began, inspired in large part by the exceptional natural beauty of the countryside.) As the leaves tumbled, they strewed the forest floor with foliar confetti, leaving elegant skeletons dressed in bark of a thousand subtle colors and patterns.

One small tree (or large shrub) fascinated me by blooming with a piercing and far-reaching sweetness as the rest of the woods lapsed into slumber. I loved the teasing quality of this scent, which would arrive on the wind, catching my attention, then play tricks on my nose. Now strong, now faint, it changed strength and direction constantly as I tried to follow it. Once I figured out that the smell was coming from a certain tree, I was amazed that such a potent scent could come from such tiny and curious-looking flowers.

These late-blooming blossoms belonged to the native autumn witch hazel, *Hamamelis virginiana* (slowly, to 30'). Multitrunked and shrubby in form, this little tree has bold, rounded leaves that turn a clear old gold in autumn, then fall away to reveal the slim-petaled red-and-yellow flowers that cling to its slender fingers like swarms of silky little insects. The blossoms open in October and November, when flowers of any kind are very welcome, however small. I like to cut armloads for the house, where their fresh, clean sweetness fills a room most pleasantly, reminding me of the old-fashioned witch hazel astringent New England women used to clean their faces.

In the Northwest, autumn witch hazel grows well in shady woodland gardens and in more open mixed borders as well. Buy plants in fall, looking for those that have dropped their leaves before they flower. In some forms, the foliage is too clingy, refusing to let go; this dims the brightness of the floral display, which is subtle at best and needs all the help it can get. Good companions will help, such as fluffy *Cryptomeria japonica* 'Elegans', a strokable, small, slow-growing tree that looks like an evergreen cloud, or steel blue pillars of Port Orford cedar, *Chamaecyparis lawsoniana* 'Columnaris'.

Himalayan Balsam

*A*utumn offers relatively few but intense scents, and orchestrating them effectively becomes an increasing challenge. Any scent, of course, can be appreciated on its own merits, but in a few cases synergy turns a pleasing scent into a stunning one. In my garden, the most enticing of fall fragrance combinations is created by surrounding the English shrub rose 'Windrush' with a crop of tall, annual Himalayan balsam.

'Windrush', also sold as an Austin hybrid, is a particularly good rose for Northwestern gardens, for not only does it flower in repeated bursts from May till frost, but its glossy, healthy foliage rarely suffers from black spot or mildew. The big, semidouble flowers open from deep yellow buds into pale, buttery blossoms with the gentle yet strong scent of tea roses. Where winters can be cold, it's best to stop deadheading the roses, instead allowing the formation of the large, coral red hips. Not only are they very beautiful (and appreciated by birds), but hip production triggers changes in the plant that prepare it to face cold weather, thus reducing the amount and severity of winterkill.

The Himalayan balsam (*Impatiens glandulifera*, also called *I. roylei*), is an enthusiastic annual that has

naturalized throughout the Northwest, decorating damp ditches and roadside meadows as well as gardens. When given plenty of moisture, this industrious plant may exceed seven feet, looking more like a bushy, branching shrub than an annual, with great, toothed leaves up to eight inches long. In less optimal conditions, this balsam is smaller in every part, but will still be smothered in flowers from early summer well into autumn.

The fat little flowers of Himalayan balsam look something like a Regency bonnet with a high brim and tumbling feathers.

These flowers are fascinating when closely examined, looking something like a Regency bonnet with a high brim and tumbling feathers. The top petals are fused into a curling shield above flaring lower petals that are curiously hinged, like little swinging doors that allow hungry bees to forage in a bulbous pollen sack reminiscent of a lady's-slipper orchid. Most blossoms are pink, rosy purple, or lavender, but the strain I grow runs clean white with lemon freckles. Recently Thompson & Morgan have developed a seed strain that extends the palette from ivory and cream through solid or bicolored pinks to wine reds and dusky purples.

If you lean closer to these flowers to watch the bees at work, you catch a strong whiff of sweet, wildling perfume. Interestingly, this merely hints at a potential that doesn't fully develop until the cooler days of fall. Like musk roses and certain honeysuckles, Himalayan balsam smells more potent from a distance, because its fragrance is potentiated by air. When oxidized in autumn, it becomes exceptionally complex, so that walking down a path lined with balsam is like entering a bath and scent shop. Blended with the fragrance of the 'Windrush' roses, the result is a haunting, lyrical, living perfume that ranks among the richest of autumn's rewards.

Gold Band and Oriental Hybrid Lilies

ate lilies are very much part of the autumn garden, for several of the most fragrant species are usually still in flower in September. Chinese gold band lilies (*Lilium auratum*, to 5'), are generally still in flower in early fall, pouring out their heavy, insistent scent both day and night. Their outsized, curling blossoms look like the crinolined ball gowns of some spoiled Southern belle. Dazzling white satin petals are ruffled and rippled, each trimmed with a shimmering golden ribbon, their wide skirts scattered with glowing rubies. They tremble on their tall stems like debutantes responding with nervous excitement to their first rush of societal admiration. Gold band lilies require rich, well-drained, acid soils and a warm, sheltered position, preferring partial or dappled shade to harsh, hot sun. (For more information on culture requirements, see Chapter Three, "Summer Fragrances.")

Gold band lilies are parent to many delicious hybrids, notably the very fragrant Orientals (3–5'), which bloom from late summer into fall. Most of these are less temperamental and demanding, appreciating any good garden soil that is neither sodden nor bone dry. As its name suggests, 'Omega' is one of the latest to arrive, opening fat buds into clean white blossoms suffused with hot red. Where softer colors are wanted, sugar pink 'Antonia' makes a confectionery companion for the muted, gold-spangled 'Rose Elegance' or the white, pink-ribboned 'Muscadet'.

The rubrum lily, *Lilium speciosum* var. *rubrum* (3–6'), might fairly be called the spectacular lily, as its Latin name suggests. This splendid Chinese species is another parent of the Oriental group, and though tricky to please, where conditions are favorable it is definitely

worth growing. 'Red Champion', a selected form of this handsome lily, dates back to the 1860s, when excellent specimens of *L. speciosum* were first made available to American hybridizers. Some eighty years later, Northwestern bulb growers took this temperamental beauty in hand, crossing it with gold band lily and several other species to produce a new race of hardy, healthy late bloomers. None, however, have more grace than the straight species, *L. speciosum*, its satiny petals a true crimson mossed with deeper, blood red spots. The starry heart of each fragrant flower is a glowing grass green edged in white, centered with little explosions of cinnamon-tipped stamens. There are other forms as well, from ice white 'Album' to scarlet *L. S.* var. *gloriosoides* or the fresh raspberry sorbet of *L. S.* var. *rubrum*. All are stoutest and most lastingly successful where summers are warm and winters mild.

Tea Olive

Lots of people confuse tea olive, *Osmanthus* × *fortunei* (6–15'), with holly. Indeed, this glossy, compact evergreen shrub does look quite similar, but it has a party trick that common holly can't beat. In late summer and fall, tea olive produces clusters of small, creamy flowers that freely spill their heady, romantic sweetness through the garden. In the maritime Northwest, this handsome shrub performs best when sheltered from biting winter wind by house walls or companion trees and shrubs. Allow it plenty of room to spread its wings and it will slowly build into a lovely, shapely plant. (At the back of a crowded border, it tends to be more of a green lump.) Tea olive grows well in full sun or partial shade, preferring rich, humus-enhanced soils. Its dam, *O. heterophyllus*, is more compact and slower growing, making it a better choice in small gardens. It has a number of attractive forms, including 'Variegatus',

with creamy edges to its dark green leaves, and 'Goshiki', a splashy one with coppery pink and salmony tints on the new leaves and lemony lime mature foliage. All also offer late bloom and lavish fragrance.

Phlox

The piquant, slightly musty smell of phlox takes me straight back to childhood, where it grew with New England asters and brown-eyed Susans. Some people detest this smell, and I admit it has decidedly rank overtones, yet it is overall a happy one, with a heavy floral base like that of snap-dragons, mixed with sweet grass or new-mown hay and honey. So there's a hint of decay thrown in—after all, the garden itself begins in manure and ends in compost. What true gardener will protest when fra-grances contain both high and low notes? It is true, though, that phlox are not notable fragrance mixers, combining well with very few scents (sweet alyssum is a winner, as are a few roses such as semidouble, strawberry-ice-cream-colored 'Dapple Dawn' and the clear rose single 'Kathleen Mills').

Border phlox are horribly prone to mildew in dry soils, but newer strains are more resistant.

Though many border phloxes begin to flower in midsummer, some are later on the scene, not hitting their stride until the approach of fall. Most are hybrids between *Phlox paniculata* and *P. maculata* and a few other, less fragrant species, so they are not equally gifted with scent. (This is especially true of orange, salmon, and reddish flowered phlox, most of which are all but scentless.) Reliable late bloomers that are so gifted include 'Russian Violet' (30") and dark pur-ple 'The King' (to 30"), both long bloomers that combine beautifully with blue and lavender asters. For clean white,

try 'Mt. Fuji' (to 3') and 'David' (to 42"). (The latter takes a break, but repeats in September.) Very tall 'World Peace' (to 45") and 'White Admiral' (to 3') are both outstanding performers, especially in retentive soils.

Buddleia Mint

Certain flowers putter along quietly all summer, then gain brilliance and clarity of color as well as depth of fragrance as autumn approaches. Buddleia mint, *Mentha buddleiafolia* (also called *M. longifolia*, is such a plant, one that I always threaten to uproot in summer but forgive in fall. This strong grower was given to me by dear friends whom I later came to suspect of duplicity when their deceptively lovely present revealed astonishing take-over tendencies. Velvety leaves and stems are tipped by long panicles of darkly fragrant soft purple florets, which, like the fuzzy, grey-green leaves, give off a powerfully minty smell, fresh and zesty. In summer, the flowers have a softer odor, like mint tea with lots of honey. In fall, however, they seem saturated in scent, their aromatic qualities definitely in the ascendant.

Seduced by those fluffy mauve-and-purple flower heads, I allowed this silver-frosted thug to wander at will through a large border. Unchecked for a whole year, it ran with a vengeance. When I realized what had happened, I filled a large garden cart (nearly six cubic feet) with the roots produced by that single slip of a plant. Thick, white, and squarish, they were so tightly interlayered that they had choked out a host of worthier companions without compunction. These days, I grow buddleia mint along the driveway, where frequent incursions by the UPS truck keep it at bay. This mint will grow very nicely in a large container, but must be divided and given fresh soil every year or it will look limp and exhausted rather than lusty. It combines extremely happily with the piquant scents of feverfew (currently named *Chrysanthemum parthenium*) and lavender.

Roses

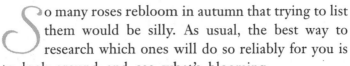

So many roses rebloom in autumn that trying to list them would be silly. As usual, the best way to research which ones will do so reliably for you is to look around and see what's blooming well for friends and neighbors and in nearby nurseries. Next, take some home and try them yourself. First among my own favorites is an ancient Chinese rose called 'Yue Yue Fen' (which supposedly means "monthly pink"). In England, where it is known as 'Old Blush' or the monthly rose, this almost everblooming rose has been beloved since its introduction in 1793, but its history in China goes back over a thousand years. Well documented in paintings as well as poetry, this loosely doubled, soft pink rose blooms as generously for gardeners in the Pacific Northwest as it did for the Prince of Heaven in the Imperial gardens. In beds and borders, the monthly rose makes a bushy, relatively tidy shrub that can easily be kept to three or four feet. Given a warm wall to warm her old bones, she will stretch to eight or ten feet, covering herself with flowers for most of the year.

The monthly rose 'Old Blush', given a sunny corner, will bask like a cat, producing crumpled pink blossoms all year long. ❧

'Old Blush' is not, you will note, called the daily rose—nobody can say this rose is never out of flower. It will, however, produce the odd blossom all through the winter (rather more where winters are mild). Naturally, this isn't always so—during the harsh winter of 1990, 'Old Blush' had quite a few flowers until the mid-December Arctic Express arrived, taking out buds that would have bloomed in January and February, as well as most of the

older canes. Thank goodness, such experiences are not the norm, and most years, we can count on having flowers or fat buds of 'Old Blush' to decorate holiday tables from Thanksgiving to Valentine's Day, as well as during the normal rose season.

Feverfew

Another inexhaustible flower, the humble feverfew, *Tanacetum parthenium*, is often a monthly bloomer, except when hard winters nip its tight green buds. If plants are kept deadheaded, a steady supply of these buds will unfailingly appear all through the autumn, opening at intervals into bright-faced white daisies with hot yellow centers. They have a brisk, astringent sweetness with a bit of a peppery bite to it, a delicious antidote to the mild silkiness of sweet peas or velvety roses. I like to mingle feverfew with an unusual fall-blooming perennial called *Strobilanthes atropurpureus* (to 5'). This looks very like a huge, upright nettle, decked each morning with dark blue-violet flowers (these look borrowed from the salvia family), which fade and fall by afternoon, to be replaced next day by a new batch. They have a sharp, nutty, slightly dusty fragrance that reminds me of fall and bonfires, also combining well with the more pungent chrysanthemums (bronze and tawny orange ones look especially nice). In warm years, feverfew will still be flowering happily at Christmas. In colder ones, the buds stay tightly shut, looking like fat green pincushions, until a burst of those sunny, warm days so common in January lures them open to feed the first hungry bees.

Chapter
Five

WINTER
SCENTS

December, January,
February

Although winter is the quietest of garden seasons, it is the quiet of reflection and replenishment rather than the stillness of death. For thousands of years, people have been holding midwinter revels, celebrating the solstice victory of light over darkness. That little corner of time, tucked between the dark end of the old year and the bright beginning of the new, is a period during which we almost instinctively examine the past and plan for the future. (This is probably the ancient source of the traditional impulse to make New Year's resolutions.) As the great seasonal tide of the year pauses at the ebb before rolling on toward summer's fulfillment, we too are poised in a small stillness, the turning point for people and plants alike. From now on, every day will be a few minutes longer. After this long night passes, buds begin to swell on shrub and tree, while underground, root and bulb start to stir. The return of the light brings a renewal of spirit to the gardener as well, reawakening our desire to create, to make, to achieve.

Time out of mind, people have brightened these darkest days of the year by bringing the outdoors inside, recognizing that living greenery lifts spirits and elevates moods. Our Northern European ancestors trimmed huts and halls alike with holly and mistletoe, and ashes left in ceremonial lamps indicate that cave dwellers in the more distant past used herbs and plants to chase away the demon winter. If folk in warmer climes had less reason to fear the dark, they still celebrated the return of the sun with green leaves and bright branches, aromatic herbs and fragrant flowers.

Indoors, of course, anybody with a window can have a galaxy of splendidly scented plants on parade all winter long. Gardeners who have discovered the delights of forcing (perhaps we should call it "coaxing," which has a less bullying sound) bulbs can fill the house with flowers during the holidays. The newer Israeli paperwhites (narcissus) boast enormous heads of silky flowers with an almost overpowering perfume. Clean white 'Ziva' has a mysterious fragrance, tinged with musk and myrrh, while a butter-and-egg-yellow bicolor, 'Bethlehem', smells like wildflowers and honey. Chalky yellow 'Nazareth' and creamy 'Omri' produce large flowers with potent but gentle perfumes that scent a room with delicacy and grace. Older paperwhites are still well worth growing, particularly the ancient Chinese sacred lily, a narcissus whose small white and gold flowers have a fascinating incenselike fragrance, and citric yellow 'Soleil d'Or', which smells softly spicy.

Northwestern gardeners are particularly blessed, for we can enjoy an abundance of blossom, berry, and bark indoors or out with very little effort. While mild years are always the most rewarding in terms of quantity, lots of off-season bloomers will make an appearance no matter how chilly the winter. Nearly all winter flowers are strongly scented, a fact that is rarely obvious until a warm, sunny day proves the point. On typical chilly days, one has to actively seek out the usually pen-etrating scents of witch hazel (*Hamamelis*), sweet box (*Sarcococca*), or winter honey-suckle (*Lonicera fragrantissima*). Curiously enough, fragrance is often inversely pro-portionate to the drama of a winter bloomer; the most insignificant plant in looks may be extraordinarily gifted with scent. One may be hard put, for instance, to locate the wispy white flowers of sweet box, despite the flood of scent they release, while the skinny yellow scraps of witch hazel flowers look far too small to produce the saturated sweetness of their lilting winter perfume.

Winter perfumes are often wanderers, straying far from their sources to captivate unsuspecting gardeners.

It's wonderful fun to seek out winter-fragrant plants, following leads in literature, exploring gardens,

and experimenting with unfamiliar plants. A neighbor and an adventurous gardener, Diane Dwyer, pointed out that a Japanese aster relative, *Gymnaster savatieri*, which is occasionally offered in local nurseries, smells powerfully of green apples even in the depths of winter when the plant is largely dormant. Familiar plants may similarly reward us during the off-season. We all know that creeping mints and thymes smell wonderful in warm weather, but may be surprised by the richness of their winter scents when we brush their slumbering mats with cold fingers or muddy knees as we weed.

Sweet Crocus

If few people realize that certain snowdrops and crocus are fragrant, it's probably because few people have occasion to put their noses next to these diminutive blossoms. I admit that cold mud and slush are daunting, yet those of us who continue to putter in the garden all year round are invariably tickled by such little treats as the ripe grape fragrance of tommies, *Crocus tomasinianus*. Those willing to descend to their level will also learn that the milky blue buds of tommies are licked with gold at the base, giving the blossoms a luminous inner glow. From their hearts rise three tangerine-colored stamens, fluffy with pollen, and three golden pistils, ready for the first bees. Early in January, the tommies are opening in pale blue puddles beneath our elderly birch tree. These are quick workers, for over the past eight years, a few dozen bulbs have multiplied into more than a hundred. In an older garden nearby, ten bulbs planted in the 1920s by my neighbor Margaret Ward (who is still gardening at ninety-three) have colonized into hundreds, spangling the grass under a huge old vine maple like a thousand living amethysts.

Other markedly fragrant crocus include the charming golden *C. chrysanthus*, an early-blooming (usu-

ally mid-February) species with a host of named selections like yellow, purple-streaked 'Advance', 'Cream Beauty', and black-and-white 'Ladykiller'. Many were chosen by that great English gardener E. A. Bowles, who called them after favorite birds like 'Snow Bunting' (whose strongly fragrant white cups have porcelain blue markings on their silky backs) or opalescent 'Blue Bird'.

A beautiful Greek species, *C. laevigatus*, is a true winter bloomer, often beginning in late November and carrying on till March. Although they were once rare, recent strides in tissue culture are making these little bulbs readily available, so more people can appreciate the fruity scent of their stippled white cups, which are feathered with purple on the inside and mahogany outside. Still hard to find, chartreuse *C. leichtlinii* releases the woodland sweetness of wild primroses in midwinter, while a couple of Italians, the lilac-and-biscuit-colored *C. suaveolens* and the larger, showier *C. imperati*, pour out their passionate perfumes (honeysuckle mixed with primrose) shortly thereafter. You won't find these sweet things at the corner garden center, but they do show up at regional plant society bulb sales, and can be had from specialty mail order nurseries as well.

Vibrant Viburnums

ander through the garden in January, after gentle, soaking rains have melted away a lingering layer of ice, and you will discover that already, in these first weeks of the new year, the softening ground is beginning to release that enticingly green scent of spring. The beds are full of twittering birds feeding companionably on the seed heads of spent perennials. Robins and thrushes poke about amongst the moldering leaves, hoping to find worms and sleepy bugs. The gardener is also pleased to see the worms but is longing for other signs of life, a promise that true spring really is on the way.

Well-furnished gardens offer all sorts of such signs, not only precocious flowers but fabulous fragrances as well. Perhaps the sweetest and most penetrating of winter perfumes streams from *Viburnum farreri* [*V. fragrans*] (to 10'), a deciduous Chinese shrub related to the great honeysuckle clan. In spring, when the new leaves are tinged with bronze, and in summer, when they are lustrous dark green, *V. farreri* makes an unobtrusive background shrub. In winter, however, its faults are laid bare. Indeed, it becomes quite hard to overlook its essential shapelessness. Just when you are wondering why you planted it, this unprepossessing shrub begins to open its tubular little flowers, and all is forgiven. These blossoms (which look very like lilac) appear at the stem tips in little tufts, opening from rosy buds to clean white flowers with an outrageous fragrance. I use this and similar viburnums at the back of mixed borders, where they make a quiet green screen in summer, but if you don't have room for such a lumbering creature, look for the dwarf form, 'Nanum', a compact two-footer with the same sumptuous scent.

Shaggy in looks, generous in flower, and splendid in scent, Viburnum burkwoodii offers white blossoms tinged pink in the bud. ❧

A close cousin, *V. burkwoodii* (to 10'), is similarly dual-natured, being shaggy (especially when young) in looks yet generous in flower and splendid in scent. Its white flowers are flushed with pink in the bud, nicely set off by the bronzed purple of its winter foliage. In truth, this effect is more pleasing in a table decoration than in the garden (this is one of those semievergreens that usually looks a bit scruffy in winter), but the smell of the flowers is deeply satisfying anywhere. Indeed, the honey-and-spice smell of *V. burkwoodii* is many people's favorite winter perfume. Some writers also praise

Burkwood viburnum for its fall color (old leaves turn hot orange before they fall), but this is so patchy that it often looks more like death throes than a salute to autumn. All these caveats don't mean this plant isn't worth growing; its decided charms have earned it a respected place in many gardens. What it does mean is that we think well about that place, giving this (and other viburnums) helpful companions that will set off its strengths while masking its weaknesses.

Confectionery Companions: Viburnum and Clematis

*I*n my garden, a shaggy old laurustinus (*Viburnum tinus*) comes into flower in early January, its clustered, pale red buds opening into loose tufts of tiny ivory flowers that smell nicely spicy on the chilly air. (Don't cut them for the house, though, because the scent turns catty in the warmth. Indeed, most viburnums are better enjoyed out of doors than in, where the flowers either shatter early or change their scent, developing a candy sweetness with slightly nasty undertones.)

If not the sweetest smelling of the viburnums, leathery, evergreen laurustinus is among the most lastingly attractive. It also makes an excellent and welcoming host for a winter-flowering fernleaf clematis. Diminutive and pretty, this scrambler has never achieved wide popularity—perhaps because of its often-changing, always unwieldy name (*Clematis cirrhosa* var. *balearica*). In a mild year, its creamy, delicately scented bells may appear from November into March. When blizzards or hard frosts occur, the plump buds continue to swell until they look like tiny balloons, yet they may not open fully until February. The wild primrose smell of this lacy clematis softens the rather obvious scent of the laurustinus, the two combining on the air into a simple but pleasing perfume that's nicer than either one on its own.

Fragrant Flowering Plums

By mid-February, the native Indian plum (*Oemleria cerasiformis* [*Osmaronia cerasiformis*], to 10'), which lines city alleys and country roadsides alike, has already opened. Its drooping sprays of creamy flowers look like miniature cherry blossoms tucked beneath leaves as upright as cats' ears. Indian plum's flowers have an unusual smell (like baby powder mixed with male cat spray), as do their leaves, which smell exactly like freshly cut watermelon if you crumple them between your fingers. Happily, others of their rose-family relatives make up for this lapse of good taste.

For one thing, the thousands of ornamental plums (*Prunus* spp.) that fill suburban yards and city sidewalk strips are nearly always in bloom by late winter, scenting the air with their distinctive fragrance. Most ornamental plums smell as sweet as rose-clan cousins like cherries, apricots, and apples. Like apple blossom, flowering plums have a light and decidedly floral fragrance. They vary in intensity, but all plum perfumes have spicy overtones, combining the sharp warmth of cloves and the slight mustiness of mace with a hint of mellowing nutmeg.

Among the nicest of the early-flowering plums is *Prunus cerasifera* 'Newport' (to 25'), which offers single pink blossoms and dark purple leaves. In February, decked in its frothy pink flowers, this round-headed tree seems to float above the garden like a fluffy, fragrant cloud. The flowers appear before the leaves, which emerge coppery purple and deepen to burgundy before fading to ink green in midsummer. A sport (a natural mutation) of 'Newport' called 'Mt. St. Helens' has even richer, longer-lasting foliage coloration. This one also develops into a handsome tree (if not disfigured by bad pruning).

A very high percentage of flowering plums have purple or red foliage. Unfortunately, most are rather homely trees for much of the year. Many look awkward if not ugly in winter silhouette, then become sullen and lumpish in summer. Their brief transformation into blossoming beauties doesn't always outweigh these drawbacks, but threading them with clematis can help a good deal. Summer bloomers like sea colored *Clematis* 'Multi Blue', red-and-purple 'Royal Velvet', or lavender 'Will Goodwin' look smashing when set off by masses of murky foliage.

My own favorite is the Japanese flowering plum, *Prunus mume* (12–20'). These graceful trees have been grown for centuries in Japan, where named forms abound and the winter Plum Blossom Festival celebrates the delicacy of their scented flowers. Japanese plum grows well in the Pacific Northwest, blooming in midwinter in mild years. Upright but spreading and many-branched, *P. mume* can get leggy, but with careful pruning it develops an interestingly twisted shape, becoming a striking specimen in border or lawn.

Neither a true plum nor an apricot nor a peach (though called all three), mumes bear large and lovely flowers with a firmer petal texture than most fruit blossom. Exceptionally fragrant and persistent, the cupped flowers last from late winter into spring. In summer, many mumes will bear good crops of hairy, rather tasteless little fruits that look deceptively yummy.

A number of excellent named forms of *P. mume* were developed early in this century by Walter Clarke, a well-known nurseryman from California's Bay Area. To this day, 'Rosemary Clarke' is considered the best of the white-flowered mumes. Rosemary has large, loosely double blossoms with vivid red calyxes, their open hearts filled with long and silky stamens. Her sister, 'Peggy Clarke', is very similar, but with deep rose petals. Peggy's buds and blossoms are particularly frost hardy (unlike

Rosemary's, which can be damaged by frost or windburn). A favorite with the bonsai crowd, 'W. B. Clarke' is a weeping mume that spills in a soft tumble of double, warm pink flowers in late winter.

Peggy also makes a pretty tree, arching and graceful in form. Like many other mumes, Rosemary is best treated as a large shrub. For remarkably abundant bloom, cut her (or other mumes) back every few years. Instead of having a central trunk, the plant becomes a rounded, many-armed shrub. Removing most of the older branches allows the younger growth plenty of light and air, which results in an ardent and prolonged flowering period. Plants will stay healthy longer if just half or a third of the stems are cut hard (to under one foot) each year, with the remaining ones trimmed back by half.

Where winters are gentle, the mumes will begin to flower in January and continue until March. In colder climates (and colder years), the mumes won't start flowering until late February, but may carry on into April. Whenever they arrive, their enticing, spicy perfume adds a delightful touch of warmth to a chilly winter day.

Wintersweet

A graceful, slow-growing shrub, wintersweet (*Chimonanthus praecox*, 8–12') is even more excitingly perfumed than Japanese plum, and perhaps easier to place in small gardens. After a warm summer, this cascading shrub fills house or garden with its emphatic scent of spiced honey and lime. Cupped and translucent, the dainty, drooping little flowers are palest yellow with ruddy hearts, popping open in pairs or small clusters at the tips of the golden-brown stems. Modestly attractive in summer, wintersweet's gleaming, dark green leaves make a pleasant backdrop for a small clematis (but choose one that can be whacked to the ground in fall so that the winter display isn't marred by clutter). In autumn, the green leaves turn soft shades of gold, spilling in quiet confetti across the lawn. Young plants take their time about blooming (a seven years' wait is not uncommon), but gardeners with patience and a sunny, sheltered spot (south-facing walls are the usual suggestion in England) will find this choice creature to be a treasure that grows more welcome with each passing winter.

Witch Hazel

Another winter bloomer that will fill a room with a wild and pungent perfume is witch hazel (*Hamamelis*). A small clan with only five members (there have been as many as thirty at various times—oh, those busy botanists!), these chunky shrubs or small trees have bold, rounded foliage that colors dramatically in autumn. Tiny and twisted, the strange flowers are not showy, but in several species boast a remarkably pleasant and carrying scent. Elegant in every season, the witch hazels have a natural grace that makes them fit comfortably into gardens of all kinds, whether formal or cottagey or outright wild. Though the most popular hybrids (a group known as *H. × intermedia*) can be quite colorful in flower (remember, this is in winter, when anything counts), many lack the distinctive scent that makes certain species invaluable to the fragrance gardener. My particular favorite is the Chinese *H. mollis* 'Pallida' (15–30'), a handsome, strapping winter bloomer with thready flowers with petals like strips of watered silk, pale yellow and amber. In the maritime Northwest, these woodland shrubs thrive in full sun, where their foliage takes on dazzling sunset hues, but they also do well in light or dappled shade, particularly if this comes from deciduous neighbors so that the witch hazels receive plenty of light in winter.

Boxleaf Azara

In my garden, *H. mollis* 'Pallida' (which, by the way, is based on the word "pallid" and so is pronounced with the accent on the first syllable, not the second, as one so often hears it) is partnered by a pair of deliciously kitchen-scented shrubs, boxleaf azara and sweet box. I don't know why more people don't grow boxleaf azara, *Azara microphylla* (slowly, to 30'), because everybody who smells this glossy evergreen wants one. True, it isn't the showiest shrub around, and young plants are very slow to put on bulk. Only in the warmest Northwestern gardens will it reach tree size, being periodically cut to the ground by frost in most places. (This winter pruning is actually helpful, encouraging a bushier shape.)

Azara recovers from winter damage quickly once established, its flat, boxwoodlike branches soon reweaving their tracery of green across a southern wall or fence. It flowers in flushes, from late fall until early spring, when the undersides of the branches are whiskered with minute brown flowers that look like nothing but smell like nothing on earth. In the garden, the fragrance seems more like ethereal vanilla, but indoors, it suggests supernal chocolate. Either way, the scent is heavenly, especially when paired with that of sweet box, which is complementary in value, so the two seem to slide into one another, creating a series of related (and delectable) scents in the process.

Sweet Box

Larger of leaf than azara, the Himalayan or Chinese sweet boxes (*Sarcococca*) are also glossy evergreens, but these are dapper little things, the largest of which will comfortably fit into the smallest

garden. This is *S. ruscifolia* (slowly, to 6'), a slim, upright shrub that spreads in very slow thickets in bed or border, or can decorate a wall with grace and dignity. Blooming in mid- to late winter, its pendulous little white bell flowers are inconspicuous but intensely and deliciously fragrant, their scent carrying on the air for a considerable distance, particularly on still, warm winter days. The most common species is *S. hookeriana* var. *humilis* (to 18"), a compact shrublet that makes fat little cushions of gleaming green, decked in winter with tiny white flowers and in summer with gleaming, inky berries. A number of other species and forms are occasionally to be found in regional nurseries; all are lovely and well worth trying, and all will give generously of their mega-vanilla and spice-cookie scent. All kinds of sweet box grow well in shade (even deep, full shade) if given decent soil. They benefit appreciably from an annual feeding mulch of aged manure and compost, remaining presentable and well groomed all through the year.

Blooming in mid- to late winter, the pendulous little white bell flowers of sweet box are inconspicuous but intensely and deliciously fragrant.

Delicious Daphnes

No fragrant garden should be without a few winter-blooming daphnes, for their exceptional scent, deep and warm, makes a rich base for numerous living perfumes. Each species smells a bit different, but all have a similarly syrupy quality, like honey thickened with brown sugar and thinned with orange-flower water. My particular favorite is winter daphne, *Daphne odora* (to 4'). When I make a new garden, this bushy little Chinese evergreen is one of the first things I plant. Though quirky, it often thrives in

maritime gardens, smothering its shiny leaves beneath masses of tubular, rose-and-cream flowers from midwinter into spring. Where it doesn't do so well, it's well worth trying again, putting new plants in several different microclimates, for this is a willful little thing that grows where it pleases, not by the book. The finest plant I ever had grew between a sidewalk and a concrete stairway, basking in dry soil and loads of reflected heat and light. It also grows happily in the shade of a large purple hazel, and again at the edge of a dry meadow in half shade. The secret (if there really is one) seems to be offering winter daphne lean but humusy soils that are very well drained. Like so many winter bloomers, this one is so potent that a single sprig picked for the house can scent a whole room.

The mezereon, or February daphne (*D. mezereum*, to 4') is a deciduous early bloomer with a sumptuous scent similar to that of *D. odora*. To my eye, however, it is far less lovely, being leggy and coltish, its hot pinky-purple flowers clinging to bare stem and twig in a graceless, not to say lumpish manner. Many people adore it, however, and nobody can deny that those bright blossoms are remarkably endowed with the familial fragrance. It blooms, as the name suggests, from late winter into spring, growing best in light shade and deep, humus-rich soils. Its fat purple buds need shelter from biting winds, or they may get blackened before they open.

Oregon Grape

Some winters, a string of gloriously sunny days call open buds of all sorts unusually early. This January, I was visiting Margaret Ward, an island gardener now in her nineties, whose tiny seaside garden is never without something in berry or bloom. As I approached the house, my nose was teased by a drift of intense, slightly lemony sweetness. Sure enough, the

Oregon grape (*Mahonia aquifolium*) in her dooryard was starting to open its sunny yellow blossoms, long before those in my shadier garden were ready to awaken.

Oregon grape is not always such a precocious bloomer, yet this evergreen shrub is a reliably distinctive presence in the winter garden. The lacquered luster of its hollylike leaves reflects gleams of light, brightening shadowy corners. From autumn into spring, the leathery foliage takes on tints of claret or burgundy that look pleasantly warm on chilly, grey days. As winter fades, the fragrant flowers unfold—rumpled, semidouble rosettes in thick clusters of clear, cool yellow. These are succeeded by plump berries of midnight blue with a pewtery bloom that makes them look like little Concord grapes. The slightly sweet fruits were traditionally used for jam and, by coastal peoples, as a meat seasoning, but they are now chiefly valued for attracting birds to gardens.

Native Oregon grapes make excellent garden company—hardy, beautiful, adaptable, and easy to please. ❧

As the common name implies, Oregon grape is a native Northwesterner, common from British Columbia into California. Tough and handsome, it makes the transition from meadow and wood to garden with ease. The species tends to be upright and a bit lanky, but judicious annual pruning keeps this glossy shrub dense and well clothed. Wild forms may exceed six feet in height, but numerous compact cultivars are available that make excellent, naturally low candidates for hedge or border settings.

M. aquifolium is a variable species with lots of lovely offspring. My friend Margaret's plants were dug from the woods over forty years ago, but these days, local nurseries can offer all sorts of improved forms. Although the species itself offers the ruddiest winter foliage (particularly when sited in full sun), *M. a.* 'Orange Flame' boasts brilliant, coppery new growth that matures to dark green

in summer, then turns smoldering ember red in winter. The muted green foliage of 'Atropurpurea' turns the murky, subfusc red of old port from fall into spring. A form called 'Moseri' offers a prolonged display of color changes, with winter tones of smoky bronze giving way to a pale, satiny green that deepens at last to rich spruce in summer.

If all these color changes leave you queasy, a fairly new Dutch selection called 'Smaragd' (this sounds scary, but just means "emerald") remains an appropriately saturated, fresh grass green all year long. A relatively dwarf selection, 'Compacta' (about 2'), also stays green most of the time, with a brief flush of red on the new leaves in spring. Shapely and nicely rounded, this one is a good choice for smaller gardens. It has especially small leaves on short internodes (the bits of stem between the leaves), giving it a neat, fine-textured appearance.

Margaret's garden is open and sunny, with a full southeastern exposure, so her plants are always in flower before mine. However, Oregon grape is not a shy bloomer in shady situations. Indeed, it tolerates a wide variety of conditions with aplomb. Plants grown in deeper shade can become scraggly in time, but this fault, as well as any tendency to lankiness, is readily corrected through pruning. Any that are markedly taller than the bulk of the plant can be cut back hard (to within a few inches of the ground). New growth will bounce back surprisingly soon, so don't worry if the plant looks a bit lopsided just at first.

Weak or scrawny stems will fatten up nicely if you encourage them by picking the flowers for the house. Feel down the stem a few inches below the blossom clusters and you will find a rough, slightly thickened area. Cut the flower stems off here and your plant will respond with lush new growth. Continue this for a few years, and a thin, misshapen shrub will turn into a sleek and well-clad one.

Ordinary soil of almost any type is acceptable to this stalwart shrub, which is highly drought tolerant once established. It is probably worth mentioning that this phrase does not mean that you can buy young Oregon grapes, jam them into a dusty garden pocket, and walk away. It means that you still have to water new or young plants for a couple of years, but once they get their roots well into the soil, they can survive on natural rainfall.

Sweet Winter Iris

For most gardeners, the big bearded border beauties define the iris clan, but these beloved perennials have dozens of cousins, as varied in season as in looks. Indeed, with a bit of research, one can find iris species that bloom during almost any month. Several very easygoing ones are both fragrant and winter-flowering, and if their flowers are less splashy than those of their summery kin, they are all the more welcome for appearing during the dark side of the year. A strappy little Algerian, *Iris unguicularis* (to 12"), is a perennial with flattened storage roots (rhizomes) something like those of the border irises. Though evergreen, its broad foliage grows in such untidy tufts that this unprepossessing plant always looks decidedly informal. It isn't a front-of-the-border star, yet when it produces a long succession of softly fragrant, gently tinted flowers from late fall through the long winter, its physical imperfections are easily overlooked. These flowers are often dismissed as inferior to those of summer iris, but they have the charm and grace of many wild plants, their subtle coloration and lovely markings in no way less beautiful than more buxom border beauties.

Partner winter iris with evergreen herbs like rosemary and lavender for winter company.

∾

Their arching standards may be silvery blue, mauve or light purple, the flaring, diamond-shaped falls often a shade deeper, with cheerful golden bands running from white throats. Once called *I. stylosa*, these iris do indeed have notable styles (the three little forked-tongue-like bits that stick out from the center of the blossoms, rising between the falls and the standards), dusted all over with glittering gold.

First and longest in flower is *I. unguicularis* 'Walter Butt', a hard worker who delivers a steady stream of powdery blue, ripe-plum-scented blossoms from Thanksgiving until Valentine's Day, often continuing into March after a warm summer. Most other Algerian iris are not so obliging, not beginning to flower until after the winter solstice. Long popular in England, they are less known on this side of the water, perhaps because they thrive only here in the Pacific Northwest. Regional nurseries offer a number of named forms, including violet-blue 'Mary Barnard', with relatively large and colorful flowers, sea blue 'Oxford Form', green-striped 'Alba', and 'Winter Treasure', which is more valued for its strong scent than for the color of its numerous but slightly dingy flowers. Many people say winter iris smell like fresh grapes. To me, the light, soft scent is indeed fruity, yet it smells simply like spring. To fully experience the fragrance, pull (don't cut) the long-necked flowers while they are still tightly furled and bring them in the house. They will open slowly in the warmth, their scent growing stronger as they do.

Algerian iris prefer poor, gritty and dry soils in open, sunny positions. Where summers are cool, they grow best at the foot of a south-facing wall, where they receive reflected heat and light. Perfect drainage is a must, but these tough little survivors produce far more flowers in lean soils than in rich ones. Resist the impulse to feed these lean creatures with commercial fertilizer, or all you will get for your kindness is lots of scraggly leaves and few flowers. On very acid soils, a mixture of aged manure and agricultural lime will be of more use than plant food, for these iris perform best in neutral or rather limy situations. Most garden books insist that these iris need no manure or compost. However, I find the plants do better over the years when given a moderate annual feeding consisting of organic soil amendments rather than potent commercial fertilizers.

More Fragrant Iris

Mild midwinter thaws often coax the first flowers from another sweet winter iris, a little bulbous one called *Iris reticulata* (6"). Diminutive but powerfully fragrant, these flowers are also so boldly colored that a clump of a dozen will carry visually clear across the garden. The species itself is rare in gardens, where named selections—most in vivid shades of blue and purple—are more common. Given an open bit of ground, reasonable soil that does not receive supplemental summer water, and plenty of sun, these small iris persist for many years, often slowly increasing into little colonies. Clear, warm yellow *I. danfordiae* is similar in size and shape, but less permanent in garden settings, where blooming bulbs are replaced by dozens of baby bulblets that rarely make it to maturity. If it is deeply planted (four to six inches, rather than the recommended two to three inches, below the soil surface), this common problem can often be avoided. These iris have a scent like sweet violets, but bright with high notes that violets don't have. Indeed, they both smell and look very nice indeed when grown in partnership with sweet violets, as well as with scented primroses.

A Fragrant Climber

Those who visit Seattle's Northwest Flower and Garden Show in February are dazzled not only by the visual displays but by an abundance of

natural perfumes. As the warmth of the crowd raises the temperature, marvelous flower scents fill the air. Among the most obvious is that of a vividly fragrant climber, *Clematis armandii*, a hardy evergreen with leathery, long-fingered foliage, slim and dusky, that remains strikingly handsome all year. In late winter, this Chinese scrambler sports among the largest blossoms of all the early-blooming clematis, its broad petals cupped about a cluster of pale golden stamens. White or creamy, the flowers are delectably scented, especially when the temperature rises above the 40s.

In cold or windy gardens, Clematis armandii *needs a warm, sheltered spot out of direct east light in winter, which can make frozen leaves explode.*

Lusty and vigorous, *C. armandii* needs to be planted where it can throw its long arms over a sturdy fence or trellis. Even with annual pruning, this expansionist vine will readily reach fifteen to twenty feet each season. Indeed, where space permits, it will scale trees to a height of thirty feet. If height is not your goal, a single plant can be trained out sideways to cover a whole wall, which it will accomplish in short order. This is a great way to mask an ugly house or garage, adding charm while artfully concealing architectural flaws.

Like many species, *C. armandii* is variable, and seed-grown stock may have small, rather dull off-white flowers. Two selected forms are reliably beautiful: the rosy buds of 'Apple Blossom' open into large flowers blushed with pink, while 'Snowdrift' is a heavy bloomer with clean white flowers. Both have the same perfume, which is vanillalike with light, lemony overtones that keep it from cloying. Both also have coppery new foliage that sets off their blossoms to a nicety.

All armandii clematis bloom from late winter into spring, and can be grown and pruned in the same

way. To please them, site plants at least four or five feet away from the wall (or the base of the tree) you want them to scale. No clematis likes dry roots, and all will grow best when given a huge, deep hole, well fortified with plenty of organic soil amendments. Manure and compost will provide the fluffy texture clematis roots appreciate. They also help hold the extra water those thirsty roots demand. Clematis love fish meal, but so do cats, so use whichever plant fertilizer works best for your situation. Clematis are greedy, so it helps to give them a timed-release fertilizer like Osmocote during the summer as well as a spring feeding of raw bonemeal or alfalfa pellets.

Lots of people get nervous about growing clematis because they aren't sure how or when to prune them. Like most species clematis, *C. armandii* can be grown without any pruning at all. This is most practical and pleasing when the vine is trained upward into a large, mature tree toward the back of the garden. When grown closer to eye height, or placed where they will be intimately viewed, it's better to prune these vines on a regular basis. Otherwise, the unsightly remains of last year's foliage will definitely mar this year's floral display.

This annual pruning is done in late spring or early summer, to give the vines plenty of time to put on new growth before winter. To keep plants compact and tidy, trim them back to a main framework. Choose one or more leaders—strong, central stems—and some stout laterals—side growth—for the framework. As soon as the flowers fade, remove all the tired old stems that clutter up your framework, leaving only those that look healthy and attractive.

When mature plants have been neglected for a long time, they may come to resemble tangled old rats' nests. If such a plant doesn't seem to have a healthy, good-looking main frame, whack the whole thing to within a few feet of the ground. Mulch around the root zone with a generous helping of blended soil-feeding ingredients

like aged manure, rotted compost, and raw bonemeal to encourage new growth. Water the plant liberally all summer, and by the next winter your revitalized vine will perfume the garden with hundreds of fragrant stars.

Winter Honeysuckle

Not a vine, though rambling enough in its way, lanky winter honeysuckle offers its scintillating scent at the right time of year to get our attention. Indeed, were shrubby *Lonicera fragrantissima* (6–8') to bloom in high summer, it would probably be rare as hens' teeth in gardens, where it would be crowded out by a dozen better species. In winter, however, its potent and far-reaching scent commands both attention and respect. Place this puppy at the back of the border, where its matte blue-green foliage will make a pleasant if unexciting backdrop for perennials in summer. Though evergreen (semideciduous in cooler climates), this is one of those plants that is not at its best in winter, when its lax brown stems are usually covered with tatty old leaves that are distinctly worse for wear. When the creamy flowers start to open (which can be anytime between December and February), we are willing to overlook its lack of good looks for the sake of their light, lemony sweetness. To create a singing series of interwoven scents, underplant winter honeysuckle with sweet box and winter daphne. The ever-changing combinations that result will delight the fussiest fragrance lover all winter long.

Sweet Violet

Dense tuffets of sweet violet, *Viola odorata*, clothe the garden floor even in winter, when their leaves and even their stems are mildly fragrant, particularly on plants grown in lean soil and fairly sunny sites. These sturdy little perennials come into flower very

early, often shortly after New Year's but occasionally in time for Christmas or solstice parties. Those first flowers, small and huddled, seem darker in color than their summery counterparts. They also seem remarkably strongly scented, perhaps in contrast to the sharp, slightly bitter smells of cold air and wet leaves. I usually discover the first sweet violets when weeding hands have stirred their leafy blanket, sending puffs of their soapy scent across the border. In one spot, a highly fragrant, porcelain blue violet called 'John Raddenbury' has run in a wide ribbon beneath the feet of a hardy and odoriferous lavender called 'Fred Boutin'. On sunny winter days, Fred and John create garden synergy, coming together in fragrant and memorable partnership.

A Floral Aside

I close this chapter not with any particular plant but with a plea for closer connection to the natural cycles of the year. Those who shun winter gardening as uncomfortable and messy are missing out on some of the deepest pleasures our pastime provides. Though flowering plants have a certain glamour, they are not the essence of what we are about here. Flowers are what draw many of us in to garden making, speaking as they do of love, of sex, of fruitful reproduction. Gorgeous as they are, however, flowers are not why we become lifelong gardeners. What keeps us involved is more active than mere floral fascination or even the appreciation of beauty. It is even more than the creative outlet garden making offers us. What hooks us so solidly is the experience of genuine connection with the real world, the reality that existed long before humans. Our passion may begin with roses—or lilies, or even lowly marigolds—but it soon spills over into doing and being. Doing service to our plants, being in the garden: that is the nourishment our spirit craves. If roses capture our hearts, even winter

weeding, that humblest of chores, has at least an equal power to transform the willing into devoted love slaves of the goddess Flora.

Weeding is an undervalued activity, perhaps because, like so many routine household tasks, it never ends. This perpetual quality can make it feel like a chore, but it is also a chance to get—or stay—in literal touch with our plants as well as with the earth. Enclosed by mature trees, my own garden is shady all year around, so I often spend those heavenly, sun-drenched winter days weeding at a friend's seaside garden. Open and windswept, it is saturated with the smell of evergreen herbs—thymes, rosemary, lavender, and sage—mingling with the scents of salt sea and warm fir needles. The soil feels fluffy to my fingers and as warm as bathwater. You can almost hear the little shoots and bulb snouts sighing in relief as gentle hands free them from the grip of old leaves and tangled grasses.

Although my work basket is full of tools and I own more pairs of gloves than a debutante, freshly softened soil is too delicious to resist. It feels deeply healing to touch the earth—perhaps especially so in winter, but really, this is true in every season. I am always mystified by people who experience this as "getting dirty." The first weeding of the year is an important ritual that must be performed with naked hands. Naked, our fingers can fully savor the renewal of direct contact with the soil. Naked, they can feel the new leaves, whether fuzzy or leathery or silken. Naked, they reconnect us with the life force that is the very heart of gardening.

Weeding, that

undervalued

activity, provides us

with the opportunity

to get in literal touch

with our plants as

well as with the earth.

Chapter Six

6

NIGHT-
FRAGRANT
PLANTS

ew experiences in life offer more enchantment than wandering through a garden on a still summer evening. The borders are full of little rustlings and chirps, all the small sounds of plants and birds settling in for the night. Bats and swallows swoop black across the tenderly translucent sky, chasing after clouds of fleeing mosquitoes. The cooling air is still body-warm, and each small breeze embraces the wanderer in giddy bursts of perfume from lily and jasmine, tobacco and stocks.

As the tired red sun slips below the horizon, light and color drain slowly away. At dusk, pale flowers begin to phosphoresce, gleaming like silvery ghosts of themselves. Many gardeners have noted that white or creamy flowers are peculiarly visible in the twilight, but other colors, too, share this trait. Flowers of blue, lilac, and mauve also glimmer in fading light, as do most yellows and sherbety shades of apricot, peach, or salmon.

Twilight is what the French call "the blue hour"—a dreamy time, quiet and still. There is an intimate, confidential quality to twilight anywhere, but it is especially pronounced in the garden. As the stars gain strength, or when the moon rises, the pearly light creates a shifting chiaroscuro that transforms our border beauties into changelings, weird and wonderful and quite unlike their daytime selves.

The scents of evening and night are different as well. As dusk deepens, we begin to notice subtle odors that are masked in daytime by the bolder fragrances called out by the sun. When the sun goes down, a host of mysterious smells come stealing forth—lilting, changeable aromas that tantalize the nose. We lift our faces, suddenly aware of some fascinating and half-recognized smell. If we search the beds, seeking the source of this strange emanation, we may be amazed to learn that a common plant has a brand new scent.

Fragrances can alter dramatically after dark, perhaps because of changing temperature or light. Many perfumes we know well by day become unfamiliar by night. Honeysuckle and sweet woodruff, petunia and tuberose—all have deeper or more delicious odors in the dark. Some, like Himalayan balsam (*Impatiens glandulifera* [I. roylei]) and musk roses, have a perfectly pleasant scent at close range but smell fabulous from a distance. As their volatile perfume blends with the air, it oxidizes, developing exceptional complexity and depth. This process occurs in the daytime as well, but night fragrances have added qualities that make them both memorable and indescribable.

A number of perfumed plants slumber by day and awaken by night, like wild tobacco, *Nicotiana alata*, which opens its white, hauntingly fragrant trumpets at dusk, when the moths that pollinate it are on the hunt. Since the creatures of the night don't even see color, most night-fragrant plants don't dress up for dates. Indeed, the majority have insignificant or dull-looking flowers by day. Faded lavender or washy grey, dappled green or dingy brown, these retiring creatures definitely do not grab the eye at the nursery. Indeed, many of them droop or remain tightly closed when the sun is out, coming into their own only when evening shadows stretch long across the garden. Night-scented stock, for instance, looks positively dowdy by day, when its muted mahogany blossoms are rolled up like little umbrellas. By night, however, it looks quite different, holding its head high and pouring out its staggeringly delicious scent with gay abandon on the warm, dark air. If nurseries stayed open till midnight, this night owl would be enormously popular, but because its charms are so easily overlooked in day-

Since the creatures of the night don't even see color, most night-fragrant plants don't dress up for dates. ❧

light, you can almost never find it for sale. Luckily, it's quite easy to grow your own from seed in order to experience the heady, floral champagne of its perfume.

Night scents are more wayward than their daytime counterparts, yet night-fragrant plants can be arranged (if not precisely orchestrated) to create certain sequences. Incredibly romantic effects—charmingly sweet and innocently promising—may be produced by planting sweet peas, tobacco (*Nicotiana*), and stocks together. For quite a different experience, place pots of petunias and tender, tropical daturas or species of *Brugmansia* on the patio. To most visitors, their intriguing jungle perfumes sing strongly of lust and passion (for me, this effect is always tempered by certain medicinal undertones that remind me forcibly of cold cream). For a more subtle, yet soul-stirring, experience, interplant the big Himalayan balsam among long-blooming 'Windrush' roses. This results in an astonishing tumble of scent that defies precise analysis but is both seductive and deeply satisfying.

It's enormous fun to play with evening fragrances, actively seeking your own ideal blends and mixtures. You don't have to have country acres to indulge this hobby; even those with pocket-hanky gardens or tiny urban balconies can put together a tub or a hanging basket of night-fragrant plants. Try night-scented stock with white petunias (these smell much nicer at night). Poke in some flowering tobacco, and add a few Chilean snowflakes (*Schizopetalon walkeri*) if there's room. Place your container where you unwind in the evenings, then notice how the ensuing perfume alters the ambience when you get home from work. Socko or subtle, such home-made aromatherapy can be both relaxing and alluring.

Laurel Spurge

In my own garden, the first strong evening fragrance arrives in late winter (usually February), when laurel spurge (*Daphne laureola*, 3–5') opens its little green buds into tubular chartreuse flowers. This naturalized native European shrub rises in tidy, whorling mounds along roadsides and at woods' edge throughout the maritime Northwest. It is also fairly common in older, shady gardens, though sadly neglected in new ones. Probably this is because few gardeners shop for plants in late winter, when this modest plant is at its best. Faint by day, its delicious daphne perfume increases from midafternoon till dusk, becoming both potent and pervasive by nightfall.

Admittedly unprepossessing compared with showier bloomers, laurel spurge is decidedly garden-worthy. Always dapper, it makes a fine addition to evergreen plantings near dooryards and entryways. In such a position, its lovely scent can be appreciated daily over several months. That quality alone makes it a treasure in late winter, when any promise of spring is very welcome, but it is a quietly pleasing creature at any time.

A European garden escapee, laurel spurge's knock-out scent makes it welcome anywhere.

If laurel spurge has a fault, it is a tendency to legginess, particularly when grown in deep shade. Even young plants may present a lot of bare stem before the whirling leaves appear, and this propensity increases with age. Fortunately, its scent is one that needs to oxidize before it can be properly admired, so the solution is quite simple. Don't give these retiring plants a front-line position, but place them behind compact, evergreen companions that remain well furnished to the ground. Many of the smaller border rhododendrons would do this nicely, as would arching sprays of *Leucothoe axillaris*, or even sturdy sword ferns. Since the flowers of laurel spurge don't smell like much up close and are too small and green to be of much visual value, nothing is lost and much is gained by placing the plants this way.

Dame's Rocket

*E*arly spring brings a number of delicious fragrances, including those of Japanese plum and winter cherry, Oregon grape and sweet box, wintersweet and witch hazels. Though none of these are solely night fragrant, all offer delicious perfumes that can be appreciated after dark as well as during the day. For true night fragrance, however, the best candidate in my garden is dame's rocket, *Hesperis matronalis* (to 3'). Here in the Northwest, the first blossoms of this old-fashioned lettuce relative often open in April, continuing to appear in flushes well into autumn. Sometimes called dame's violet because of the melting sweetness of its scent, this modest-looking plant has been cherished in gardens since the Elizabethan age. A sturdy survivor, it is often found in overgrown or long-abandoned gardens, fighting its way through weeds and grass to lift its pale flowers to the moon.

Old-fashioned flowers like dame's rocket and perennial moon-weed have been grown in gardens grand and small since Elizabethan times.

Dame's rocket is related to wallflowers and cabbages and the bitter-hot salad green known as rocket, and its white or chalky lilac flowers have the distinctive crucifer family look, being four-petaled and grouped in long, loose clusters, much like the deeper purple ones of annual moonweed (*Lunaria annua*), which

flower at the same time. By day, they smell softly of sweet violets, but as evening draws near, their scent strengthens, enriched and deepened by hints of clove and nutmeg.

Dame's rocket blooms abundantly in shade as well as in sun, growing well under a wide range of garden conditions. It is very easy to grow from seed and self-sows quite willingly. Don't weed out all the babies, for older plants grow woody and less floriferous in time, so it's worth keeping a few younglings on hand to replace their elders as they fade away. Loose in line and very casual in appearance, dame's rocket is not a plant for the front of the ornamental border. Since its scent carries well, it can be tucked into odd corners or used as a backdrop for showier companions. Place it beneath winter plums (*Prunus mume*) or under early-blooming apple trees to create delightful duos of early night scents.

Perennial Moonweed

From April on, the perennial moonweed, *Lunaria rediviva* (to 3'), breathes out its gentle perfume on the evening air. This, too, is a plant that is seldom seen except in older gardens, but unlike dame's rocket, this one would be considered garden-worthy anywhere. Seedlings build quickly into impressive, good-looking plants, generally flowering in the second year. The bold leaves, lightly toothed and drooping, are arrow-shaped at the top of the stems and heart-shaped at the base. The large, loose sprays of white or pale lilac flowers have very little smell on cold days, and only a mild one on warmer mornings, but by evening, a warm, slightly spicy sweetness is released that travels enticingly through the garden. Even at its height, the perfume is delicate at the source; it is yet another fragrance tone that blossoms only on the air.

A steady bloomer from March or April into June, if deadheaded often, perennial moonweed will bloom on in fits and starts all summer and into fall. This moderate self-sower is most apt to reproduce in young gardens with plenty of open ground space. In crowded, mature borders, you may need to save seed to grow on if you want more plants. Ordinary, decent garden soils of any kind will please it, as will moderate amounts of supplemental water. Moonweed is very drought tolerant once established, yet it blooms longer and more abundantly when given a small but steady supply of moisture.

Night-Scented Gladiola

*J*une brings a flock of night sweets, among them the pale, drooping flowers of *Gladiolus tristis* (to 24"). This dainty species has flat, strappy leaves and short, curving stems of slim, tubular flowers, creamy and slightly green on the outside but stained with wine red and lemon yellow at the throat. Though its Latin name sounds rather morose (*tristis* means sad or sorrowful), in botanical terms it signifies a plant that is most fragrant at night. (Apparently, the implicit sorrow refers to the muted colors and downcast affect of most night-fragrant flowers.)

In this case, the flowers are open-faced and cheerful, with a potent if sporadic fragrance. It is a perfect plant for maritime gardens, for it is especially free with its scent on cloudy, grey days. Dusk awakens its full powers, and on warm, dark evenings, its murky, singing sweetness pervades the garden. Now that white gardens are old hat, the next cool thing is to have moon gardens, in which all the flowers are pale colors that phosphoresce by moonlight or starlight. This night-fragrant white beauty is clearly born for a stellar role in such a garden, but will also be a welcome addition to container plantings placed where you sip your evening tea.

Though most bulbs prefer dry soil, this one hails from the South African wetlands, so give it deep, retentive soil and plenty of water when in active growth. Like any bulb, it may rot if kept overly wet while dormant, which in these parts means making sure it isn't waterlogged in winter. A good handful of grit will help open up tight clay soils that may get too wet for comfort during the off-season. These little bulbs also do very well in pots, which can be wintered over in a garage or a cold greenhouse to keep the bulbs dry during dormancy.

Datura

Evening-scented datura, deadly poisonous yet outrageously flaunting in fragrance, can literally intoxicate those who smell too much of it. Last spring, friends who were cleaning out their greenhouse gave me a large collection of these tender South American plants. Their dangling apricot-and-peach-colored bells are enormous, swirling like Ginger Rogers's skirts, extravagantly gorgeous and sumptuously scented. I grouped them by the seats we use in the evenings, where we are often joined by friends. I was commenting that our summer gatherings had been especially hilarious and wonderful lately, when a knowing botanist explained that the cause was more likely the datura than any sudden increase of wit and charm on our parts. The very scent, he explained gently, is a mild euphoriant. Sitting beneath the curving arms of a datura, inhaling the ripe effulgence of those peachy bells, one becomes a bit—just a bit—high. Not schnockered, mind you, but definitely in an altered state. At first this took me back a bit—I loved the idea that middle age brought with it a renewal of the

The very scent of this party plant is a mild euphoriant. Sitting beneath the curving arms of a datura, inhaling the ripe effulgence of those huge, peachy bells, one becomes a bit—just a bit—high.

party-animal spirit lost since young adulthood. On second thought, I felt how delightful it was to have a party plant. Even when we aren't feeling "on," the daturas perform with panache. The performance pressure is off, but the parties are better than ever.

Quite a few daturas (and related *Brugmansia* species) are available these days, both from specialty nurseries and from local garden centers. Both single and double forms abound, whose dangling bells may be cream or white, yellow or orange, lilac or deep purple. There are even some variegated forms, though these tend to look ill rather than illustrious. The apricot-colored Ginger Rogers model I favor is currently known as *Brugmansia* × 'Charles Grimaldi'. Widely grown in Northern California, it is nearly always treated as a tender shrub to be wintered over indoors elsewhere in the maritime Northwest. Treated as such, plants can be brought out of doors in late spring. Cut back any lanky branches to encourage bushy new growth, then repot in fresh soil. You can prune back the roots of plants that threaten to get too large, but they thrive in surprisingly small containers. Last year, an eight-foot plant produced over 75 blossoms at once, and then rebloomed cheerfully, while growing in a five-gallon pot.

I bring my plants into the kitchen for the winter, where they thrive so long as they are kept above 65°F. Given plenty of water, ample light, and a steady supply of fertilizer (add half-strength commercial food with each watering), they continue to bloom all winter. If you can't offer winter protection indoors, an unheated garage or sun porch will do fine. The plants will retreat into dormancy without adequate heat and light, but will rouse again come spring, when you can take them back out of doors. Ginger (or Charles) is actually root-hardy in Seattle, although garden plants won't bloom until late summer or early fall. Protected pot plants are far more generous in their bloom, so finding a place to store these big beauties over the winter is worth a bit of effort.

A shrubbier, low-growing hybrid called *Datura meteloides* 'Evening Fragrance' (3–4' in width) is a splendid pot plant for the patio. Happy plants produce endless supplies of big, upfacing flowers like outsized morning glories, white with lilac picotee edging, above large and slightly felty blue-grey foliage. As the name promises, they are powerfully scented at night. This one is really easy to grow from seed, and it will bloom the first year if given lush treatment. Daturas are also very eager rooters, and the smallest cutting will be blooming for you in no time flat.

Native throughout South America, daturas have been sacred plants for millennia. They (and the related *Brugmansia* species) are classed as entheogens, plants that allow humans to experience godhead. Poisonous in every part, they may produce a lasting visit to eternity when used without discretion. Don't mess with the foliage, bark, or roots, however much you crave enlightenment, but do enjoy their intoxicating fragrance, which spreads through the evening garden (or the kitchen) in enticing streams.

Honeysuckle

*Y*ears ago, every little house had a climbing honeysuckle somewhere, often clambering through an apple tree. Such a tree is a good place for these scrambling vines, which rarely deserve the hard pruning they get when expected to stay confined to a miserly little support fan. They also do well in their other classic position as a garden entry plant, trained over a wide, trellised arch or a sturdy gatepost.

Simply sweet by day, the night fragrance of honeysuckle alters with time and temperature and perhaps other factors we don't yet even recognize. ❧

By day, the fluffy tufts of flowers have a pleasantly floral sweetness, the fruitiness of which is apparent only when you bury your nose in the blossoms. As evening draws in and the air cools down, the fruit scent gains power and begins to steal through the garden in drifts, teasing you by disappearing as you try to follow it to the source. The night fragrance of honeysuckle is complicated, mysterious, even enigmatic—it alters with time and temperature, and perhaps with other factors we don't even recognize.

Among my favorites for evening fragrance is a long-blooming form of English woodbine. Lusty *Lonicera periclymenum* 'Graham Thomas' (to 30') will swarm up a fence or fruit tree or even a Douglas fir in just a few seasons, covering its host with a light blanket of blossom in recurring bursts from May into November. (The heaviest bloom periods are June and October.) Mine has laced through a huge quince into a 'Golden Transparent' apple tree, where the creamy yellow flowers look especially pretty surrounded by fat yellow apples. From May onward, the vine is a solid curtain of blossom that fills the garden with clouds of fragrance both early in the morning (when it is rather light and floral) and again at dusk, when the scent is rich and satiny smooth.

Honeysuckles are quite easy to please, wanting only decent garden soil and moderate amounts of supplemental water in dry summers. Like their fellow climbers, the clematis, they appreciate a cool, damp root run. Don't plant them too close to their intended host, where root competition and dry soil will slow their progress, or too close to a wall or fence, where dry conditions generally prevail. Deep mulches will help conserve moisture and keep the honeysuckle roots cool all summer, suppressing competitive weeds at the same time.

Jasmine

All romantics must have a jasmine in their gardens, but even emotional moderates will derive enormous pleasure from this quintessential fragrance plant. Like honeysuckle, jasmine smells very nice by day but becomes sumptuous by night, when its heady fragrance inspires joyful sensuality. A so-called evergreen, this lacy vine often looks pretty ratty by midwinter, so is not a candidate to drape around the front door. However, it is a great one for a sheltered bower where it will receive plenty of light to coax out the earliest blossoms in late spring, yet where both it and you will be protected from battering winds and winter frosts.

Spanish jasmine, *Jasminum grandiflorum* (12–15'), has large white tubular flowers that bloom all winter indoors or all summer outside. This is a fast grower when happy, producing lots of lacy, twining leaves in opposite pairs. They have a grip like a baby, gentle but implacable, and if you let this vine wander where it chooses, it can be hard to untwine those tight coils without seriously disturbing the unwilling host. (One year, my indoor plant engulfed the vacuum cleaner. Naturally, I was loath to sacrifice all that incipient bloom, so I was forced to wait until spring cleaning to vacuum again. After that, several people in the family felt that the plant would be happier outside from then on. It is, but I can't say that I really love resuming vacuuming.)

Poet's jasmine, *J. officinale*, can reach twenty feet in time. However, in the Northwest maritime regions, unless protected by a companionable ivy or host shrub, it tends to get cut down by hard winters before this happens. The flowers of this one are small and white, with the piercing sweetness of the family. In both cases, the fragrance is highly pleasant by day, but the evening and night versions have a smoky depth and a silky finish, particularly in warm, still weather.

Fragrant Evening Primrose

No summer evening party would be complete without a tour of the garden.

❧

Famous for its familiar perfume, the evening primrose clan boasts a fair number of night-scented members. One of the nicest is a native Northwesterner, the tufted or fragrant evening primrose, *Oenothera caespitosa* (to 8"). This is a plate-shaped little perennial, much wider than it is high, with the sweetest flowers in all its highly scented family. It's terrific fun to watch the hairy little buds open—you can pick them in the afternoon and watch them burst into swirls of bloom, for amazingly big blossoms are packed into those long, tightly furled buds. The white, pleated petals have a fabulous scent, as lush and heavy as any magnolia, but cut with a lemony tang that keeps it from oversweetness. The flowers unfurl at dusk, remaining open all night and turning rosy with morning, when they collapse into limp little rags. Place these plants in lean, well-drained soil, where they get as much sun as you can offer, and they will produce fresh buds and blossoms daily from spring into summer.

My personal favorite is a Chilean species, *O. odorata* [*O. stricta*] (3'), an upright, almost columnar evening primrose whose large, lovely flowers turn from Chinese yellow to apricot as they fade. Though it has not proved long-lived in the Northwest, it sows itself about moderately, always choosing places where its wrinkled rosettes will be unobtrusive. Many times I have thought this plant to be lost, but it reappears faithfully, scenting the night with its silky blossoms. The tall, sinuous stems are ranged with long, sticky buds that open sequentially, day after day, over most of the summer and into autumn. The flowers have a light, lilting scent that is pleasing enough by day but positively sparkles by night, when it also travels freely through the garden.

Bouncing Bet

A drab little perennial soapwort, *Saponaria officinalis*, also enjoys the more felicitous common name of Bouncing Bet. Like other soapworts, this one is a bit too determined in her creeping ways for placement in the border proper, even if she were more of a looker. However, her chalky flowers look like inferior phlox, drooping off soft stems trimmed with lax leaves. The whole plant looks tired, as if she lacks energy, and one wonders where the bounce part comes in. So why bother? Because Betty is a changeling whose dowdy daylight demeanor is delightfully transformed at night, when she tosses off her fatigue, turns her face up to the stars, and pours out a fragrance that colors the night like birdsong or calling water.

Clearly, you don't let such a creature loose just anywhere, scrumptious though she may be. However, she is not the least bit demanding, and will cheerfully inhabit any sunny, out-of-the-way corner. Let her tumble through the cracks in an old rock wall, or run merrily along the sidewalk strip, or fill the awkward edge between the back walk and the driveway. You won't notice her at all by day, but by night, you'll be glad you gave her room to roam.

Night-Fragrant Annuals

NIGHT-SCENTED STOCK

The lavender, four-petaled flowers of night-scented stock, *Matthiola longipetala (bicornis)* (1'), look rather like lettuce blossom, but they open only when the sun goes down. You plant this mild-mannered annual just like lettuce, too, sowing in serial sprinkles (repeated small batches) a week or ten days apart. This assures you of a steady supply, for each individual plant only lasts a few weeks. You will definitely want to have plenty of new plants coming along, because once you experience their indescribable perfume, you won't want it to run out. Usually people say that stocks smell like cloves, but although there is certainly a strong, spicy component to the fragrance, it doesn't smell at all like pinks or carnations, which are also described as clovelike. My nose detects traces of wild rose perfume, hints of vanilla, a touch of lemon, and even a tiny bit of bitter muskiness that accentuates the overall sweetness.

The fragrance is really indescribable, and you simply have to experience it for yourself to understand why.

The classic position for night-scented stocks is under windows that are kept open at night, so their lovely smell can enter with the darkness. It starts slowly, then

Complex perfumes like that of night-scented stock are not easily described and must be experienced to be fully appreciated.

❧

comes in scented billows, ever stronger as the night wears on. It's fun to watch its effect on unsuspecting visitors, who sniff curiously as the scent begins, then breathe in deeply, then relax into their chairs, wearing expressions of profound peace and comfort.

These untidy little plants are not kempt enough for front-line placement, so tuck them discreetly about the garden, behind shrubs or large perennials that will kindly screen them from view. Stocks dislike being moved, so either sow them where you want them to flower or grow them in pots, which can be moved near favorite sitting areas as the plants come into bloom.

FLOWERING TOBACCO

An old-fashioned flowering tobacco, *Nicotiana alata* var. *grandiflora* 'Fragrant Cloud' (3'), is my nominee for Queen of the Night Garden. Actually, quite a few tobaccos could compete for the role, but I would award the lead to this selected form, whose sticky white flowers produce such stunning olfactory arias. Regal though her perfume may be, her manners are unaffected and friendly. At ease in nearly any situation, flowering tobacco blooms as happily in full sun as in light or partial shade. A moderate self-sower, she sites her seedlings cleverly, putting them where they will be very welcome. Such willing ways win the gardener's heart as fusspot border beauties rarely can, and though this old girl may be plain of face, her night splendors will earn her a valued spot in any garden.

One friend claims he feels delightfully naughty planting the demon tobacco, even if it's just to enjoy its heady scent.

As with so many annuals that self-sow, tobacco seedlings do not transplant especially well. Scatter the seed where you want plants, or sow in pots to place about the garden. Deadhead the plants often and they will bloom all summer and well into autumn. Let the last flowers ripen, then shake the seed heads around the borders to ensure next year's crop. Although the species, *N. alata*, lends her genes to many recent flowering tobacco hybrids, her perfume is not always handed down. To be sure of getting that sumptuous night scent, grow the best form, even if it means starting plants from seed. They are quite easy to grow, and once you have a good strain in the garden, you can keep it going with very little effort.

NIGHT PHLOX

Curious rather than beautiful, South African night phlox (*Zaluzianskya capensis*, to 2') is a late riser, opening its tufted flower heads only after 10 p.m. Its scent builds slowly, and the first whiffs are like the flowers, more interesting than fabulous. Indeed, the first time I tried this plant, one friend wanted to know why I was growing something that smelled exactly like pink play dough, and I was hard put to answer her. An hour later, the plant answered for itself, for the scent deepens with the dusk, gaining complexity and depth. By midnight, those of you who are still awake will find the night phlox perfume rich and full and sensuously satisfying, but this is definitely not a flower for sleepyheads.

This weird and wonderful plant is unlikely to be found at your local garden center, for few retail outlets will stock frumpy flowers like this, whatever their unseen qualities. Fortunately, there are several commercial sources for seed (Thompson & Morgan among them), so you can grow your own very easily. Once you do so, you may have to keep reminding yourself that there are serious treats in store, because this is one of the least attractive plants I know. Limp, lank, flopsy, and distinctly weedy, night phlox needs to be planted in clusters of five or six just to make what looks like one decent clump. The tattered little flowers don't really look much like phlox, but do resemble both catchflies (*Lychnis* spp.) and ragged robins (*Silene* spp.). (Neither genus is related to night phlox, but both offer several night-fragrant members). A fitful annual (which can be perennial if the year is warm enough), night phlox has burgundy buds that open into little white florets that look utterly incapable of producing such an astonishingly powerful and pleasant fragrance. Give this plant sun, reasonable soil, and moderate amounts of water, and it will do its captivating best to convince you that beauty's only petal-deep.

CHILEAN SNOWFLAKE

A compact annual, Chilean snowflake (*Schizopetalon walkeri*, 8") resents disturbance, so sow it where you want it to grow. You can also start the seedlings in divided seed trays so that the fragile root balls aren't damaged in transplanting. This plant prefers plenty of sun and rather lean soils, tumbling happily over rock walls or gravel-edged terraces. Airy and delicate in structure, it spins out in lacy circles, looking exactly like little green doilies. The white flowers are lacy as well, spangling the stems like fragrant little snowflakes. Feathery and fringed, each one is perfectly square; these are the most geometrical flowers I have ever seen. They begin to open in the afternoon, but don't spill their delicious fragrance until dusk gathers. In older garden books, writers nearly always compare this scent to almond, and it does have a warm, nutty quality, but it also has flowery overtones that smell more like almond blossom than almond essence. As the flowers mature, the scent becomes richer and takes on strong hints of coconut as well—not the ripe fruit, but the party kind, shredded and sugared, that's used to decorate children's birthday cakes.

This is an excellent little thing to tuck into hanging baskets or window boxes, especially with the old-fashioned white petunias, which smell almost peppery by day but turn sweet and silky by night. Dangling sweet peas and raspberry-scented heliotrope also make delectable companions for Chilean snowflake, and any planting that contains this combination will create a festive atmosphere on a warm summer evening.

NIGHT-SWEET

Night-sweet, *Nycterinia selaginoides* (12"), is a crepuscular South African annual whose round tan buds stay tightly shut like sleepy little eyes all day. The plants look like nothing at all in daylight, but this shy girl really flaunts her stuff when the sun goes down. As night falls, the swelling buds burst into starry white flowers, the satiny, heart-shaped petals raying out from central bosses of old gold. Slowly at first, then more and more potently, they produce a sweetly insinuating scent that suggests a scrumptious combination of Mexican vanilla and white jasmine.

If grown in the open garden, the seedlings size up very slowly in our prolonged Northwestern springs. They respond beautifully to bottom heat, however, and I have had good results starting them on top of the water heater, which always stays nice and warm. Use generously divided seed trays (I often recycle old six-packs or four-packs for this use) to avoid breaking the delicate little roots. Once the plantlets have six or eight true leaves, you can transplant them into the garden. They do beautifully in containers filled with an open-textured soil mixture. Give them lots of sun, and let the soil dry out between watering (once the seedlings are well established, naturally). This doesn't mean the plants want to be left to crisp up in the summer sun, but they do bloom better when subjected to a little judicious stress than when pampered. Night-

Whether in pots or in the garden, night-fragrant plants need handsome companions to compensate for their often mousy looks. ॐ

sweet makes an excellent companion for tuberoses, which like similar conditions, and the two scents are extremely memorable in combination.

TUBEROSE

Mexican tuberoses, *Polianthes tuberosa* (to 3'), are not really hardy in the maritime Northwest, but are definitely worth the bit of work it takes to grow them as pot plants, for few flowers pack so potent a perfume. Even in pots, these bulblike perennials tend to sulk in cool, shady Northwestern gardens, where they can't get enough sun to bring out their best qualities. If you can give them at least six hours of full sun, preferably with additional reflected heat from nearby walls, you may convince them that they are back in their sunny homeland, and they will flower for you.

Well-grown specimens make impressive sheaves of flat, grassy foliage, punctuated with stout stems, very like their Southwestern cousin, the agave. The flowers are quite similar as well, being large and creamy, with the texture of heavy silk. Happy tuberoses produce several bloom spikes, densely studded with single or double white flowers. Their romantic scent is notable enough by day, but so intensifies at night that people who are very sensitive to smells often find it overwhelming.

To lastingly please these heat lovers, provide large, deep containers filled with rich but open-textured soil. They want plenty of moisture but dislike standing moisture, so keep them consistently damp but never sodden. They are also big feeders, so add a little commercial fertilizer each time you water, or scratch a handful of timed-release food pellets (such as Osmocote) into the top inch of soil. Gradually reduce watering as fall approaches, but don't let the roots dry out completely, even during dormancy. Shelter the pots indoors over the winter, in a garage, a basement, or an unheated greenhouse. They won't need much light, but even a few degrees of frost will carry your tuberoses South of that celestial Border.

Although you can cram three or four tubers into an eight-inch pot, it's prettier to combine tuberoses with other plants in larger ones. Lots of tropical annuals enjoy similar conditions during the summer, including silvery, trailing lotus vine (*Lotus berthelotti*), which looks very pretty tumbling beneath the spiky tuberose foliage. This netted, wiry plant is actually a tender perennial, and may well winter over for you when given the sweet treatment required by tuberoses.

Appendix
One

GARDEN
PLANS
AND
PLANTING
DIAGRAMS

Fragrance in the Spring Garden

MARCH, APRIL, MAY

1. *Paeonia* 'Audrey'
2. Anemone clematis,
   Clematis montana
   'Rubens'
3. *Malus pumila*
4. *Philadelphus* 'Nuage
   Rose'
5. *Narcissus* 'Thalia'
6. *Narcissus poeticus*
7. *Erysimum*
   'Wenlock Beauty'

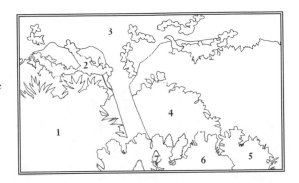

So many spring bloomers are potently perfumed that it is quite easy to create combinations that are colorful and also entrancingly fragrant. All sorts of apple trees (as well as Japanese plum or cherry) spread scented clouds above the garden floor. Early flowering *Clematis montana* 'Rubens' will weave perfumed wreaths above the garden gate. Early peonies like 'Audrey' and mock oranges such as the dainty *Philadelphus* 'Nuage Rose' will pour their perfume through the garden, mingling orange blossom and vanilla with the scent of early roses.

In many gardens, daphnes bloom from late winter into summer, their carrying odor calling to us from across the garden. At their feet bloom nodding bells of poet's narcissus, bright eyed and powerfully scented. Wallflowers such as the velvety, tea-and-toast colored 'Wenlock Beauty' blend their coaxing scents with all these splendid fragrances to make a pure and potent essence of spring.

To add early roses, consider the buttery yellow single, 'Canary Bird', with lacy foliage. Its smell is rich and almost buttery as well, with overtones of freesias and sweetpeas. To prolong the delectable experience, underplant this airy shrub rose with sweeps of fragrant bulbs. Bold blue grape hyacinths will start things off, remaining pretty and exceptionally fragrant for several months. Extend the season even further by tucking clumps of lily of the valley between clusters of fragrant narcissus like 'Geranium' or 'Actea'.

Fragrance in the Summer Garden

JUNE, JULY, AUGUST

1. *Rosa* 'Just Joey'
2. *Brugmansia* 'Charles Grimaldi'
3. *Lilium regale*
4. Giant seakale, *Crambe cordifolia*
5. *Lathyrus odoratus*

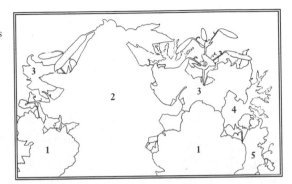

The most potent fragrance effects can be arranged in summer time, when our palette ranges from pungent artemisia to the wild honey scent of sweet alyssum. It's fun to play with timing, having scents that peak in bursts from morning till dusk. The most intoxicating scents—daturas and brugmansias, flowering tobacco—are reserved for evenings, when the garden is a haven of peace and comfort after the heat and business of the day.

Regal lilies provide one of the strongest scents in the summer garden, one that mingles deliciously with the perfumes of roses, jasmine, and peonies. Lily perfume deepens by night, as do those of sea kale, *Crambe cordifolia*, honeysuckle, and sweet peas, *Lathyrus odoratus*. Certain annuals have sumptuous fragrance both day and night. Best of these is mignonette, which means "little darling" in French, a puzzler when one just sees the frizzy, rather frumpy green flowers. Once you have grown this plant, you will never want to be without it, for despite its lack of good looks, the scent evokes dreamy romance. Cherry scented heliotrope is another prize, especially dark forms like 'Black Beauty' and 'Marine Blue', which boast dusky leaves as well as deep blue or purple fragrant flowers.

Fragrance in the Autumn Garden

SEPTEMBER, OCTOBER, NOVEMBER

1. *Gladiolus callianthus*
2. *Nicotiana sylvestris*
3. *Prunus subhiirrrtella*
   'Autumnalis'
4. *Magnolia grandiflora*
5. *Rosa* 'Dainty Bess'
6. *Tanacetum*
   parthenium
7. *Phlox* 'Miss Lingard'

The scent of fall is as crisp on the air as an apple bite. The smells of browned and tumbling leaves mingle with those of late lilies and roses. In the kitchen garden, the aromas of dried herbs, spicy tomatoes, and newly turned earth mark the end of harvest time. Dying strawberry leaves sometimes smell as succulent as their summer fruit, just as the foliage and stems of sweet violets occasionally echo the perfume of their own blossoms during the off seasons. The bittersweet hot cocoa smell of mahogany colored, late blooming chocolate cosmos speaks of the comforts of winter to come.

To weave a wondrous web of autumn fragrance and color, pair the chalky pink blossoms of long blooming 'Dainty Bess' roses with creamy swags of sweet meadow tobacco, *Nicotiana sylvestris*, fragrant ivory bells of Abyssianian gladiolus (*Gladiolus callianthus*), and clouds of white phlox like 'Miss Lingard'. Bright-eyed white daisies of feverfew, *Tanacetum parthenium*, add an aromatic twist to the blend, both from the starry flowers and from the pungent foliage. Glorious *Magnolia grandiflora* is a reliable rebloomer once established, and its huge, lemony scented flowers spill their fresh fragrance on the warm chinook, reminding us of spring even as we enter autumn.

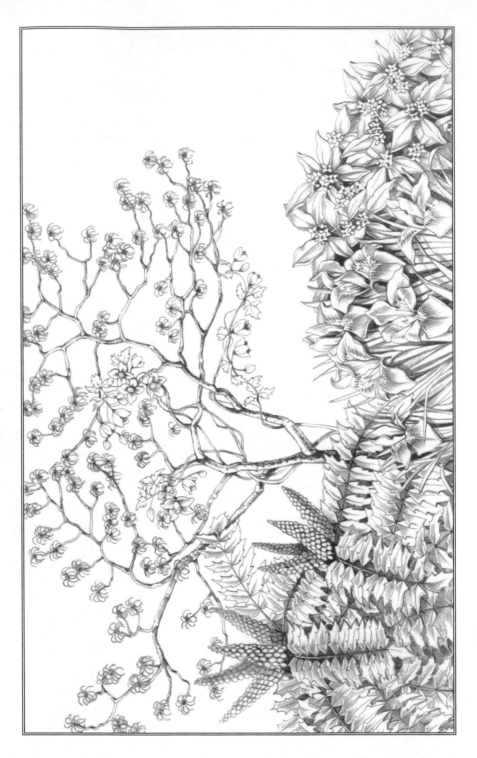

Fragrance in the Winter Garden

DECEMBER, JANUARY, FEBRUARY

1. *Mahonia lomarifolia*
2. Witch hazel,
   *Hamamelis
   mollis* 'Pallida'
3. *Clematis cirrhosa* var.
   balearica
4. *Daphne odora*
   'Marginata'
5. Winter iris,
   Iris unguicularis

Winter gardens are quiet, understated places, generally more beautiful in details than in the big picture. If winter fragrances are relatively few, they make up in potency what they lack in number. It's pleasant to place the handsomest of these off-season performers where their gentle scents will greet us daily as we approach the house or park the car. Daphnes, Oregon grape (*Mahonia*), and witch hazel (*Hamamelis*) all have far-reaching scents that penetrate the garden, carrying well even on chilly air.

Other winter bloomers must be sought out to be appreciated. The soft blue, lavender, or purple flowers of winter iris are not exactly eye catching, but when one kneels to appreciate the delicacy of their petal markings, their ripe-grape scent tickles the nose quite nicely. Lacy swags of clambering *Clematis cirrhosa* will decorate an evergreen viburnum or rhododendron delightfully, but you must bury your face in its ecru and burgundy blossoms to discover their elusive, wildling scent. One of my favorite combinations arises when the subtle smell of this clematis mingles with the deep, rich perfume of Daphne odora. In a mild year, the ambrosial result continues from mid-January until March.

Appendix Two

2

RESOURCES

Public Gardens to Visit

Quite a few public gardens have made a minor specialty of fragrance gardens. Often these are based on herbs or roses, but some of the most fascinating are designed to be appreciated by people who are blind or wheelchair-bound. Such gardens often feature plants with penetrating and far-traveling scents that can be sampled from a distance. The following public gardens offer fragrant plantings of various kinds, all of which can be explored on leisurely day trips. Though most gardens are at their peak in spring and summer, arboreta with good shrub collections will be worth visiting in fall and winter as well. For gardeners seeking plants that extend the year with off-season bloom, such junkets become voyages of discovery leading to all sorts of new loves (and sometimes to the need for bigger gardens).

For more public gardens, consult *Garden Touring in the Pacific Northwest*, by Jan Whitner, and *Visiting Eden: The Public Gardens of Northern California*, by Joan Taylor.

BRITISH COLUMBIA

University of British Columbia Botanical Garden
6804 SW Marine Drive, Vancouver, B.C., Canada V6T 1Z4
(604) 822-3928. Free October 9–March 15; seasonal fee.
Gardens open daily all year.

VanDusen Botanical Garden
5251 Oak Street, Vancouver, B.C., Canada V6M 4H1
(604) 266-7194.
Fee. Gardens open daily all year except Christmas.

CALIFORNIA

Filoli
Canada Road, Woodside, CA 94062, (415) 364-2880.
Fee. Garden open daily mid-February to mid-November; times vary, so call for specifics.

Strybing Arboretum and Botanic Gardens
Golden Gate Park, Ninth Avenue at Lincoln Way, San Francisco, CA 94122, (415) 661-1316. Free. Gardens open daily all year.

Sunset Gardens
80 Willow Road, Menlo Park, CA 94025, (415) 321-3600.
Free. Gardens open weekdays all year.

OREGON
International Rose Test Garden
400 SW Kingston Boulevard, Portland, OR 97201,
(503) 248-4302. Free. Garden open daily all year.

Jenkins Estate (herb and rose garden/braille guide)
Grabhorn Road at SW 209th and Farmington Road, P.O. Box 5868,
Aloha, OR 97006, (503) 642-3855.
Free. Garden days and hours vary; call for schedule.

WASHINGTON
Bellevue Botanical Garden
The Northwest Perennial Alliance Borders, 12001 Main Street,
Bellevue, WA 98008, (206) 451-3755. Free. Garden open daily all year.

Carl S. English, Jr., Botanical Gardens
Hiram M. Chittenden Locks (Ballard Locks), 3015 NW 54th Street,
Seattle, WA 98107, (206) 783-7059.
Free. Gardens open daily all year.

Washington Park Arboretum
2300 Arboretum Drive E, Seattle, WA 98112, (206) 543-8800.
Free. Gardens open daily all year.

NURSERY GARDENS
Nearly all family-run bulb nurseries have gardens or growing fields to tour, as do many other specialty plant nurseries. Because these are often really small businesses, your tour guide is likely to be the nursery owner. You will notice that many owners request that visitors call first even if the garden is open every day. This is not only a matter of courtesy, but a real necessity. As every mom knows, it's very hard to stay organized when one is performing a complex job while being constantly interrupted.

It's also important to be a polite visitor. If you take an hour of the owner's time, it's mannerly to buy something at the nursery before you leave. When touring nursery gardens, the same rules apply as when we visit private gardens: don't pick flowers or leaves or ripe seed heads without asking permission. Keep your feet on the paths or the lawn—even if you have a camera glued to your nose. Don't let pets (or children) run free in the garden. Don't assume you can use the house bathroom.

Though these simple requests seem like common courtesy, they are not so commonly observed as one would hope. When nursery folk seem less than excited to have company, it's probably because the last visitors were less than thoughtful and considerate. All this said, most nursery owners are in business because they love plants and plant people. Most of them are happy to talk plants with like-minded people, time permitting. If you have any doubts about whether a visit is in order, just call ahead to find out.

Mail Order Catalog Nurseries

The following list is limited to regional mail order nurseries. For a truly comprehensive overview of specialty mail order nurseries, get yourself a copy of Barbara Barton's amazing masterwork *Gardening by Mail*. Updated every other year, this magnificent book lists virtually every catalog nursery in North America as well as a good many overseas. Because Barbara is a librarian, her book is exceptionally well organized and indexed. You can find your way through it with ease no matter how you organize your thoughts. You can search by plant type—for instance, if you want remontant, or twice-blooming, iris, you will find a short list of nurseries that specialize in them—by alphabetical order, even by geographical region. (This last is a handy way to work nursery visits into vacations and business trips.)

Not all of the following catalogs offer fragrant plants only, but all specialize in them, either as such or by category (roses, violets, and so forth). Many of these nurseries are also terrific sources for companion perennials, shrubs, vines, and whatnot. Though all are mail order nurseries, many can be visited as noted.

British Columbia

Monashee Perennials
Site 6, Box 9, RR 7, Vernon, B.C., Canada V1T 7Z3, (604) 542-2592. Catalog $2.

Rainforest Nursery
13139 224th Street, RR 2, Maple Ridge, B.C., Canada V2X 7E7 (604) 467-4218. Catalog $2, $20 minimum order. Nursery open March–October, Saturdays only; call ahead. Display garden open June–August, Saturdays only; call ahead.

California

Canyon Creek Nursery
3527 Dry Creek Road, Oroville, CA 95965, (916) 533-2166. Catalog $2. Nursery open all year, Monday–Saturday.

Roses of Yesterday and Today
803 Brown's Valley Road, Watsonville, CA 95076-0398 (408) 724-3537. Catalog $3. Nursery open all year, Monday–Friday. Display garden open daily, May–June.

Shepherd's Garden Seeds
6116 Highway 9, Felton, CA 95018, (408) 482-6910. Catalog $1. Nursery open all year, Monday–Friday.

OREGON

Caprice Farm Nursery
15425 SW Pleasant Hill Road, Sherwood, OR 97140
(503) 625-7241. Catalog $2, $10 minimum order. Nursery open all year,
Monday–Saturday; call ahead. Display garden open May–September; call
ahead.

Forestfarm
990 Tetherow Road, Williams, OR 97544, (503) 846-7269.
Catalog $3. Nursery open daily all year; call ahead.

Russell Graham
4030 Eagle Crest Road NW, Salem, OR 97304, (503) 362-1135.
Catalog $2 for 3 years, or free with order. Nursery open Saturday, by
appointment only. Display garden open Saturday, by appointment only.

WASHINGTON

B & D Lilies
330 P Street, Port Townsend, WA 98368, (206) 385-1738.
Catalog $3. Nursery open daily, July–August; call ahead. Display garden
open daily, July–August; call ahead.

Collector's Nursery
16804 NE 102nd Avenue, Battle Ground, WA 98604
(206) 574-3832. Catalog $2. Nursery open all year; call ahead. Display
garden open all year; call ahead.

Cricklewood Nursery
11907 Nevers Road, Snohomish, WA 98290, (206) 568-2829.
Catalog $1. Nursery open April–May, Friday and Saturday. Display
garden open May–June, Friday and Saturday; call ahead.

Lamb Nurseries
Route 1, Box 460-B, Long Beach, WA 98631, (206) 642-4856.
Catalog $1.50. Nursery open all year, Monday–Saturday. Display garden
open all year, Monday–Saturday.

Robyn's Nest Nursery
7802 NE 63rd Street, Vancouver, WA 98662, (206) 256-7399.
Catalog $2. Nursery open April–June, also September,
Thursday–Saturday. Display garden open May–September; call ahead.

Skyline Nursery
4772 Sequim-Dungeness Way, Sequim, WA 98382. Catalog $2, $20
minimum. Nursery open all year, Tuesday–Saturday. Display garden
open June–October, Tuesday–Saturday.

Other Good Sources for Fragrant Plants

The Pacific Northwest is home to some of the finest specialty nurseries in the country, so most of us will be able to find pretty much whatever plant we are looking for regionally, if not locally. Nurseries that specialize in herbs abound in these parts, too—there are far too many to list here, but a quick skim through *Gardening by Mail* will reveal more plant sources than most of us can afford to know about. For more specific help, consult the book's Plant Sources Index under lilies or roses or whatever category to which the necessity in question may belong. Certain national nurseries that specialize in scented plants are excellent resources as well, so here are a few of the best.

Carroll Gardens
P.O. Box 310444 E. Main Street, Westminster, MD 21158
(410) 848-5422 or 800-638-6334. Catalog $2.

The Fragrant Path
P.O. Box 328, Ft. Calhoun, NE 68023. Catalog $1.

Sandy Mush Herb Garden
Route 2, Surrett Cove Road, Leicester, NC 28748, (704) 683-2014.
Catalog $4. Nursery open all year, Thursday–Saturday. Display garden open May–October, Thursday–Saturday. Call ahead.

Other Resources

LIBRARIES

BRITISH COLUMBIA
University of British Columbia Botanical Garden
6804 SW Marine Drive, Vancouver, B.C., Canada V6T 1Z4
(604) 822-3928. Judy Newton, VanDusen Gardens Library.

Vancouver Botanical Gardens Association
5251 Oak Street, Vancouver, B.C., Canada V6M 4H1,
(604) 266-7194. Barbara Fox

CALIFORNIA
Helen Crocker Russell Library of Horticulture
Strybing Arboretum Society, Ninth Avenue at Lincoln Way
San Francisco, CA 94122, (415) 661-1514. Barbara Pitschel.

OREGON
Berry Botanic Garden Library
11505 SW Summerville Avenue, Portland, OR 97219
(503) 636-4112. Janice Dodd.

WASHINGTON
Elizabeth C. Miller Library
Center for Urban Horticulture, University of Washington,
GF-15, Seattle, WA 98195, (206) 543-8616. Laura Lipton or Valerie
Easton.

Books for Further Reading

Though fragrance gardening is not a common topic, a small but
rich vein of horticultural writing exists on the subject. In recent years, several fine writers have turned their attention to fragrant plants, and there
are also a number of wonderful older books on fragrance that are well
worth seeking out. Libraries and secondhand bookstores are likely sources
for the older volumes, and the scarcer ones can often be found through a
good book search service.

This partial list includes the most accessible and practical books
on fragrance, all of which are suitable for advancing gardeners. If you have
trouble finding them in your local bookstores, try calling Seattle's
University Bookstore (206-634-3400), Flora & Fauna Books (206-523-
4727), or the legendary Powell's Books in Portland (800-878-7323).
Another outstanding mail order resource is Capability's Books in Deer
Park, Wisconsin (800-247-8154). They list some 1,000 titles (including
many older ones) and are always ready to offer great suggestions.

Barton, Barbara J. *Gardening by Mail*, 4th ed. Boston and New York:
    Houghton Mifflin, 1994.
Genders, Roy. *Scented Flora of the World*. New York: St. Martin's Press,
    1977.
James, Theodore Jr. *The Potpourri Gardener*. New York: Macmillan,
    1990.
Lacey, Stephen. *Scent in Your Garden*. Boston: Little, Brown, 1991.
Lima, Patrick. *The Harrowsmith Illustrated Book of Herbs*. Toronto:
    Camden House, 1986.
Reddell, Rayford Clayton and Galyean, Robert. *Growing Fragrant Plants*.
    New York: Harper and Row, 1989.
Verey, Rosemary. *The Scented Garden*. London: Mermaid Books, 1981.
Wilder, Louise Beebe. *The Fragrant Garden*. New York: Dover, 1974
    (reprint of original Macmillan 1932 edition).

3

Appendix
Three

INDEX